Yoga
A PATH TO WELLNESS
A WORKBOOK FOR STUDENTS

Alison Donley

SECOND EDITION

Kendall Hunt
publishing company

Cover image: Winter Dune © Michael Kahn
Interior photos taken by Rachel Donley

www.kendallhunt.com
Send all inquiries to:
4050 Westmark Drive
Dubuque, IA 52004-1840

Copyright © 2010, 2016 by Alison Donley

ISBN: 978-1-5249-6537-2

Published in the United States of America

Contents

Assessments and Journals

Introduction

It is quite possible that I have the best job in the whole world. Each semester, I am infinitely grateful for the twists and turns (pun intended) that have led me to this good fortune in my life. I am blessed to be able to share Yoga with so many wonderful students. While I may never be financially wealthy, I believe myself to be one of the richest people on Earth.

The balance and peace I have found through the practice of Yoga have been a guiding force in much of my life. All students of this amazing system owe a debt of gratitude to those who came before us to lay the foundation and forge a path for us to follow in shaping and creating our lives. I am personally grateful as well for all of the students with whom I have shared this practice so far. Through their dedication and honesty, they have taught *me* so much. I love them on the first day I meet them and I will forever.

Like most people, my path has been blocked by the occasional fork in the road, small stepping stone, or *giant* boulder. This is part of life. If we were to run away from the challenges, we would never find out who we really are. Many philosophers and theologians have speculated about this dilemma, this "human condition." An interestingly painful, yet comical, definition of this term comes from Elizabeth Gilbert in her book, *Eat, Pray, Love*. Ms. Gilbert refers to the human condition as "the heartbreaking inability to sustain contentment."

The late author, mystic, philosopher, and clergyman Alan Watts (1951) spoke about the human condition in the following quote:

> Under these circumstances, the life that we live is a contradiction and a conflict. Because consciousness must involve both pleasure and pain, to strive for pleasure to the exclusion of pain is, in effect, to strive for the loss of consciousness.

As Dr. Jon Kabat-Zinn, a pioneer in the field of mind/body medicine, so thoughtfully observed in his book titled, *Full Catastrophe Living*, life is made up of the good and the bad. The lovely and the not-so-lovely. The joyful and the dreadful. The "stuff" of life. How we choose to react to our circumstances will indeed either create or destroy our opportunity for inner peace. The first yogis recognized that a worthy mission, a mission that could lead each person toward his or her full potential, was to go inward and study the Self. Through this amazing system of self-study and self-care called Yoga, we can learn to answer some very basic questions:

Who am I? How do I function in this world? Why am I here? How can I learn to handle suffering?

When the yoga student begins to discern his or her amazing potential for balance, for wellness, the answers to these questions will often appear. The enlightenment gained on this journey of self-discovery begins to illuminate our "Capital P" Path. As we go inward in a yoga practice, we begin to learn more about how we operate in this world. We learn to be calm. We learn to breathe deeply. Like a sculptor, we begin to whittle away at our attachments, our fears, our anger, our pain…until we arrive at the masterpiece that was there all along.

Yoga has allowed me to be a better person. I think I am a better wife, mother, friend, sibling, and teacher than I would have been without this beautiful practice that helped me to treat myself with love and compassion and bring that forward into all aspects of my life. I think I was a kinder daughter than I would have been. I came to Yoga when I was sixteen years old. I would repeatedly check a book out of my local library, B.K.S. Iyengar's *Light on Yoga*. I had no idea of the beauty and power of the words in that book back then, for I did not read it until I was much older. Back then, I would lock the door to my bedroom, put a Pink Floyd album on the turntable, flip randomly though the book, and then do the best I could to get into the "pretzel poses" on the pages in front of me. As a sixteen year-old hippie-athlete, my intention was to develop my flexibility for the sport I loved. As a competitive gymnast for many years, the flexibility I gained from bending myself into the postures helped me to not only stay injury-free for competitive gymnastics throughout high school and college, but also to enhance my performance and creativity.

I do, however, often joke with my students about how much money I could have saved my parents (on therapy) had I *really read* the book when I was a teenager! As the old Zen proverb states, "When the pupil is ready to learn, a teacher will appear." I guess I was just not ready back then.

Are you?

Targn Pleiadas/Shutterstock.com

Acknowledgments

My life has been blessed with the guidance of many knowledgeable and superior teachers. Through the years I've had the opportunity and great honor to learn from some of the best: A.G. and Indra Mohan, Tim Miller, Richard Freeman, David Swenson, Beryl Bender Birch, and Jon Kabat-Zinn, to name a few. However, when asked to construct a workbook for Yoga, the task felt enormous and out of reach. The immediate encouragement and support I received from my family was the push I needed to get it started, and eventually completed. Even though my parents are both deceased, I could sense their encouragement. My dad would often say, "You will do what you will to do." As a teen, this pearl of wisdom used to annoy me and my siblings. It took me a number of years to really understand the influence these words have had on my life.

I want to thank my husband Dean for his love, support, and writing expertise. He has always given me great advice and continues to be my best friend and mentor. His help with this project was invaluable. Thanks, too, to my wonderful children, Rachel and Trevor, for their love, support, and patience. Most of what I have learned about how to live my Yoga has come through the awesome job of being a mom. How lucky I am to be theirs.

This book could not have come to fruition without Rachel's great photography and asana skills and Trevor's calm vibe. Thanks to Phil Donley for his sage advice and for his expertise through the many roles he has had in my life: athletic trainer, father-in-law, physical therapist, and friend. I wish also to thank coaches from whom I've learned patience and persistence (necessary qualities to build a yoga practice) through the years: the late Art Sanders, Bonnie Wolff, Rob Beaumont, and Sandra Thielz.

I would also like to thank the former Dean of the College of Health Sciences at WCU, Dr. Don Barr, for over a decade in support of promoting wellness; Barbara Lappano for encouraging me to create a yoga course in 1998; Em Jones, Dr. Ray Zetts, Dr. Frank Fry, Dr. Craig Stevens, and Dr. Melissa Reed for the support and encouragement they have offered through the years; and the Dean of the College of Health Sciences, Dr. Scott Heinerichs, for his vision of what the future of health and wellness can and should be. West Chester University is truly a progressive place.

Thank you to Pamela Walsh, Lori Klein and Kate Simmons for their gifts of teaching yoga. With their help, we have been able to expand our class offerings to include numerous sections of Yoga I, Yoga II and Yoga III, as well as a 200-hour Yoga Teacher Training Program. Thank you to Dr. Don McCown and Dr. Chris Moriconi, whose vision and hard work have led to the creation of a Contemplative Studies Minor at WCU which includes Yoga I.

Additionally, I would like to thank all of my students, past and present, for teaching me the most amazing lessons life has to offer.

The following West Chester University students deserve special recognition for their assistance in putting the asana practice section together: Ryan Cook, Kasi Crossan, Rachel Donley, Travis Ford-Bey, Ronnie Koons, and Kevin Trei. I would also like to thank the many yoga

teachers and students from The Light Within Yoga Studio for their assistance in modeling some of the postures.

Thanks to photographer, yoga student, yoga teacher and friend, Michael Kahn, whose photo "Winter Dune" graces the cover of this text.

A very special thank you to my daughter Rachel! I am so grateful for the time she spent to share her brilliant artwork and photography skills.

Special note: In this text, the word Yoga is purposely capitalized when the reference is to the spiritual practice as a whole and not capitalized when referring to the practice of Hatha yoga.

Within the text, the words "yogi," which means male yoga practitioner, and "yogini," which means female yoga practitioner, are in most cases combined by the use of the term yogin.

Courtesy of Alison Donley

Purpose of the Text

The focus of this text will be primarily to help you learn more about yourself as you create a fitness and wellness routine through an introductory practice of one of the systems of Hatha yoga, the physical path to union of body, mind, and spirit. We will explore modern-day Ashtanga yoga, also called ashtanga vinyasa, a profoundly transformative and therapeutic practice created by Pattabhi Jois and his guru, Krishnamacharya, also known as "the father of modern yoga". As a student of this particular system for over twenty of the forty years that I have been learning and practicing yoga, I feel a tremendous reverence to it. Ashtanga vinyasa requires austere discipline and decades of study *and* commitment to a regular practice. One of Pattabhi Jois's favorite quotes was "ashtanga yoga is ninety-nine percent practice and one percent theory." On this particular path, you cannot be an armchair yogin. To truly understand the theory, you *must* be willing to do the practice.

I have an infinite amount of respect and gratitude for all that has transpired in order for *anyone* to be able to enhance their lives through ashtanga vinyasa yoga. Reducing the practice to fit into a semester may come across as disrespectful to the system as a whole, so it is my wish to be clear that this book is intended as a guided *introduction* to this amazing practice. The fifteen-week prologue, so to speak, will be merely a seed. It will be up to you to nurture that seed to allow it to grow, if you so choose. While this system is best learned with the knowledge and guidance of a well-qualified instructor trained *specifically* in ashtanga vinyasa yoga, the brilliance of the sequences make it a wonderful primer. Typically when one learns this particular practice, he or she can take the knowledge gained to explore any other system with a definite advantage.

We all have David Swenson to thank for his creation of "short forms" of the Ashtanga Primary Series. I will be pulling from these short forms to create the section (Chapter 7) which offers the physical practice we will be exploring during the course of the semester. In addition, I will offer information particular to this method at the end of Chapter 7 for those of you wishing to continue on.

There will be days when a gentle practice may be more suitable. For that reason, a sequence with such an approach can be found on pages 124 & 125.

Some of you may be inclined to dig deeper into the practice as a whole. For that reason, most chapters will offer a section titled "Going Deeper." This small section will include homework, or "OMwork." There may be thoughts to ponder as well as an occasional suggestion of reading material to further your understanding of the concepts within that particular chapter.

The following quote is from the Introduction of a book by film director David Lynch titled *Catching the Big Fish: Meditation, Consciousness, and Creativity* (2006):

> Ideas are like fish. If you want to catch the little fish, you can stay in the shallow water. But if you want to catch the big fish, you've got to go deeper. Down deep, the fish are more powerful and more pure. They're huge and abstract. And they're very beautiful.

I look for a certain fish that is important to me, one that can translate to cinema. But there are all kinds of fish swimming down there. There are fish for business, fish for sports. There are fish for everything.

Everything, anything, that is a thing, comes up from the deepest level. Modern physics calls that level the Unified Field. The more your consciousness—your awareness—is expanded; the deeper you go toward this source, and the bigger the fish you will catch.

YOGA takes you into the present moment the only place where LIFE exists.

Art by Kaitlin Fritz

What *Is* Yoga?

Photos by Rachel Donley

"Who am J who walks, stands and functions on this elaborate stage known as the earth? J should find this out."

—Yoga Vasistha

There are really quite a few answers to the question "What is Yoga?" Yoga is both a methodology and a philosophy. According to *The Sivananda Companion to Yoga* (2000), Yoga is the oldest science of life. Perhaps one of the best quantifying answers would be, "Yoga is the perfect system of self-care," because while most wellness programs would help an individual to concentrate on, and improve, a few aspects of fitness and wellness, this particular system aims to create balance and wholeness. It targets the whole person.

Yoga practice can help you create incredible physical fitness. Just as important however, the practice attends to matters of the mind (intellect and emotions) as well as the spirit. While there are a number of definitions for the word *yoga*, simply stated, it means union: union of body, mind, and spirit. A deeper exploration of both the methodology and philosophy of Yoga often leads to an understanding of the deeper definition: oneness; union of the individual soul with Divine consciousness.

Yoga cannot be done. You can *do* yoga postures, or asanas. You can *do* yoga breath work, or pranayama. However, Yoga is a state of consciousness to be cultivated, and as such, Yoga can only be created.

In his beautiful book, *Light on Life*, B.K.S. Iyengar (2005) explains it in this way:

> "Spiritual realization is the aim that exists in each of us to reach our divine core. That core, though never absent from anyone, remains latent within us. It is not an outward quest for a Holy Grail that lies beyond, but an Inward Journey that allows the core to reveal itself.
>
> In order to find out how to reveal our innermost Being, the sages explored the various sheaths of existence, starting from body and progressing through mind and intelligence, and ultimately to soul. The yogic journey guides us from our periphery, the body, to the center of our Being, the soul. The aim is to integrate the various layers so that the inner divinity shines out as through clear glass."

A Brief Introduction to the Philosophy

Yoga helps us to understand ourselves and how we react in this world. A beautiful quote from the *Upanishads* (1987) sums it up nicely:

> "It would be easier to roll up the entire sky into a small cloth than it would be to obtain true happiness without knowing the Self."

Yoga allows us to tap into our pure potential. Using the breath to fuel the body and steady the mind, we begin to create a union between the two. In time this leads us deeper inward. Body, mind, and spirit are not separate. We are whole human beings. Too often, however, we operate in a state of disconnect. Only with a steady mind can we look at our lives—and life in general—with clarity. To paraphrase Eckhart Tolle in *The Power of Now* (1997), yoga gives us the awareness to stop paying so much attention to our life situation so that we can *start* paying attention to our life. Our life is right here and right now. This perspective gives us a glimpse both inward and outward into the beauty of our lives—a clear view of the big picture. Your life situation currently may be a mess. It may indeed be quite chaotic. It may be full of the "stuff" of life. But when you can stop and think about your life in the here and now—meaning *this* moment (take a deep breath), and now *this* moment (take another deep breath), can you really find a whole lot wrong with the present?

The practice of Yoga dates back to at least thirty-five hundred years Before the Common Era (3500 BCE). The oldest evidence of the existence of the physical practice came from stone seals excavated from the Indus Valley in 1918 by the British archeologist Sir John Marshall and his team. A number of the stone seals unearthed depict men in yogic postures and are believed to be around 5500 years old. This may mean that at least one yogic posture still recognized and practiced today was practiced for meditative purposes many thousands of years ago. The postural practices, or Hatha yoga, which many refer to as "yoga" today have likely evolved out of more modern times (Singleton 2010). Nonetheless, the findings unearthed from this ancient civilization are extraordinary. It is obvious that this was a very advanced society. It also was quite amazing that no weapons were found that would imply that men fought one another, leading scholars to believe that the people from this time period practiced non violence, or ahimsa (Sivananda Yoga Vedanta Center, 2000).

The language of Yoga is Sanskrit. It is an ancient, beautiful, spiritual, highly scientific language of sound, rhythm, and vibration that has been touted as linguistic perfection. Sanskrit has been around for at least thirty-five hundred years. The current popularity of yogic practices

throughout the world has generated an enormous interest in Sanskrit. Yoga classes often begin and/or end with Sanskrit chanting, which can be felt as pure energy throughout the body. However, chanting can be uncomfortable to many people. Upon deeper exploration of the meanings of the chants, as well as the healing power of the vibrations created through chanting, most come to love and appreciate this aspect of practice.

Some people believe that Yoga is a religion. Recently, with the rise in popularity of the practice of Hatha yoga, this has begun to be addressed more fully. Most scholars agree that Yoga most likely evolved from Stone Age shamanism, possibly hundreds of years before Hinduism. The practice was passed down orally for thousands of years before it was first recorded.

While no one really knows for sure when Patanjali documented the *Yoga Sutras*—a series of one hundred ninety-six aphorisms that are intended as a guidebook for the practitioner—most agree that it was likely around the second century BCE. Patanjali defines Yoga as the means of calming the fluctuations of the mind. The eight-limbed path to union, or Ashtanga Yoga, that Patanjali put forth in the *Sutras* includes such things as moral codes of conduct and ways of behaving; the yamas and the niyamas, which many argue constitute dogma. However, even Ishvara Pranidhana, one of the niyamas, which can be translated as "belief in, and surrender to God," can be interpreted as a belief in a power that is larger than you.

The roots of Yoga can indeed be traced through Hinduism, Buddhism, and Jainism, however, each of these belief systems viewed it somewhat differently. Most of the early spiritual texts of Yoga came to us through Hinduism, which refers to Yoga as a term meaning "yoke" and implies that one's individual soul (Atman) could yoke with that which underlies everything (Brahman). Tantric Buddhism refers to Yoga as a type of spiritual practice, according to the *New World Encyclopedia*. In research titled, "All Life is Yoga," by Pravin K. Shah from the Jain Study Center of North Carolina, Shah states, "All life either consciously or subconsciously is Yoga, meaning attempting to realize its perfection. In itself yoga has very little to do with a particular religion, but it has a great deal to do with individual spirituality and its perfection." (**http://www.fas.harvard.edu/~pluralsm/affiliates/jainism/jainedu/yoga.htm**)

According to T.K.V. Desikachar's comments about the topic, as reported by Phil Catalfo in the March/April 2001 issue of *Yoga Journal* ("Is Yoga a Religion?"), at some point in its evolution, the practice of Hatha yoga was rejected by Hinduism. This, in part, was because the practitioners of yoga would not claim a particular deity (or deities) that one must worship. The existence of God was not denied but was widely believed by the ancient yogis to be in *all things*. While Hinduism does embrace the practice of postures, breathing techniques, and meditation, it rejects the philosophy of God as an option.

There is no church of yoga, unless of course you wish to consider your body the "temple of your soul." There are no religious services, no clergy, and no sacramental rites. Yoga allows the individual to feel the "spark of Divine"; the oneness, or connectedness that comes through union of body, mind, and spirit. It asks the individual to look within. Rather than teaching you what to do, Hatha yoga helps you discover how to be.

If the prospect of yoga practice makes you uncomfortable because of your religious beliefs, perhaps answering the questions below will help calm your concerns.

- "Does my yoga practice help me feel better?"

- "Has my practice improved my health and wellness?"

- "Is my practice helping me to be a better person out in the world?"

If the answers to these questions are a resounding "YES!" then...why would you *not* practice yoga?

There are two main things that are true for *all* of us:

1. We are in this (human condition) together...and

Robert Kneschke/Shutterstock.com

2. When we learn to appreciate, care for, and love ourselves and others, we shine.

Courtesy of Alison Donley

Yoga was created thousands of years ago as the original yogis attempted to understand themselves and the world they lived in—certainly still a worthwhile intention today....

History of Yoga

The history of Yoga is a bit ambiguous, so while many of the puzzle pieces have come together, there are no clear start and end times to the early periods recorded below. Hopefully, the following information will give you some perspective into the depth and breadth of Yoga—it was compiled with assistance from Gita Desai's beautiful documentary, *Yoga Unveiled* (2004).

- Stone Age shamanism 25,000 BCE. Many academics believe that the roots of Yoga were formed during this time, a time when human beings were looking deeply into the nature of the body and the mind.

- Early Yoga/The VEDIC PERIOD 5000–1500 BCE. The Vedas were recorded during this time. These hymns reflect a period of time when humans were recognizing a deep connection to nature and began expressing a belief in a higher power. Sometime during the end of this period, likely around 2000 BCE, the first major religion, Hinduism, was formed.

- The PRE CLASSICAL PERIOD/EPIC PERIOD. During this time, the *Upanishads*, which were recorded sometime between 1500–500 BCE, helped to further the teachings of the Vedas. Also during this period (563–483 BCE), the Buddha, through his life and teachings, shared the wisdom that later became the practice of Buddhism, which has many similarities to Hinduism. The *Mahabarata Epic* was recorded as well, which includes the *Bhagavad Gita*, likely recorded around 500 BCE. Along with the Vedas, all of the revered writings mentioned above are still considered to be sacred texts of Hinduism.

- The CLASSICAL PERIOD OF YOGA. During this period, around 150 BCE, Patanjali recorded the *Yoga Sutra* and revealed the eight-limbed path of Yoga, or Ashtanga Yoga.

- The POST-CLASSICAL PERIOD OF YOGA. Around 1500 CE, the *Hatha Yoga Pradipika* was written by Swami Svatmarama.

- The MODERN PERIOD OF YOGA 1785 to present. The modern period marks the beginning of a proliferation of literature on Yoga and an increase in the teaching methodologies. In 1785 the first English translations of the *Bhagavad Gita* and other yogic "scriptures" was taken on. The marked difference in this period was that the main focus of yoga now seemed to be more on living in, and accepting, the present moment, rather than trying to transcend reality.

A Few (of the Many) Landmarks During the Modern Period

1887 Swami Sivananda was born. The most prolific yogi to date, Sivananda, a prominent Indian doctor, recorded two hundred books on yoga and philosophy. His teachings can be summed up in six words: "Serve, Love, Give, Purify, Meditate, Realize." Sivananda created the "Five Principles of Yoga," which can be found in *The Sivananda Companion to Yoga* (2000), and are as follows:

1. Proper relaxation (savasana)
2. Proper exercise (asanas)
3. Proper breathing (pranayama)
4. Proper diet (as sattvic, or pure, as possible)
5. Positive thinking and meditation (dhyana)

1888 The birth of Tirumalai Krishnamacharya, one of the greatest yogis of the modern period, often referred to as the "the father of modern yoga." Krishnamacharya lived to be over one hundred years old. In addition to being a yogi, he was an author, a researcher, a Vedic

scholar, a healer, and a linguist, as well as an expert in the Indian schools of thought. The popularity of yoga today is largely due to T. Krishnamacharya, who with his vast knowledge revived the practice in the early twentieth century. He developed and adapted yoga practices for individual students by refusing to standardize the methodology. His ability to garner the wisdom from the ancient teachings—and make it relevant to anyone with whom he worked—was exceptional. A few of Krishnamacharya's students (B.K.S. Iyengar, Sri K. Pattabhi Jois, A.G. Indra Devi, and Indra Mohan, and Krishnamacharya's son, T.K.V. Desikachar) went on to create methods that tens of millions of people in the United States alone now practice. It would be extremely difficult to find a style of Hatha yoga that was not influenced in some way by this amazing yogi.

1893   From September 11 to 27 the first Parliament of World's Religions met at the Chicago World's Fair. This group represented the very first formal gathering of spiritual traditions from the East and West. Swami Vivekananda, a Hindu yogi from Calcutta, delivered a profound and moving speech that brought the seven thousand attendees to their feet for an ovation that lasted three minutes, when he began with "Sisters and Brothers of America...."

1899   The birth of Indra Devi, often referred to as "The First Lady of Yoga." Devi was known by her students as "Mataji", which means "respected mother." She became the first woman to be admitted into Krishnamacharya's Yoga school in 1937. Devi authored numerous books and taught yoga in many different countries. She was beloved for creating a system that focused on gentleness and compassion that honored the eight limbed path of Yoga. The year before her death at the age of 102, Devi shared a profound message at a gathering of teachers and students at a national yoga convention: "You give light and love to everybody-those who love you, those who harm you, those whom you know, those whom you don't know. It makes no difference. You just give light and love."

1915   The birth of Sri K. Pattabhi Jois. Jois studied with Krishnamacharya from a very early age and was later selected by the Maharaj of Mysore, India, to teach at the Sanskrit college there. He founded the Ashtanga Yoga Research Institute in Mysore, which continues to attract practitioners from all over the world. Jois's methodology pulls from Patanjali's model of Ashtanga yoga (eight-limbed path to union) as recorded in the *Yoga Sutras*. Jois's "modern-day Ashtanga"system, often referred to as Ashtanga vinyasa, includes a series of vigorous asanas (postures) performed in a flowing manner (vinyasa) with specialized breathwork (ujayii pranayama) and muscle locks (bandhas). The first series is known as the Primary Series, or Yoga Chikitsa, which means "yoga therapy." The Primary Series realigns the spine and builds muscular strength, endurance, and flexibility. In addition to a proper diet, the strong asana and pranayama practice creates the heat for intense sweating. The full series takes about ninety minutes to complete. The Second Series, or Nadi Shodana (nerve channel clearing), is meant to strengthen the nervous system and the subtle energy channels (nadis) throughout the body. There are four advanced series called Sthira Bhaga. These series are to cultivate Divine (bhaga) stability/steadiness (sthira) and are intended only for advanced students. These practices were originally created for young boys and young men. British gymnastics and wrestling conditioning movements heavily influenced Jois as he and Krisnamacharya created this amazing practice.

   Sri K. Pattabhi Jois passed away on May 18, 2009. He left an amazing gift to the world, which will continue to be shared by his son, Manju, his daughter, Saraswathi Rangaswami, and his grandson Sharath Rangaswami, as well as the numerous teachers he so lovingly trained (**http://www.kpjayi.org**).

1918   The birth of B.K.S. Iyengar, who taught yoga for seventy years and authored numerous books on yoga and yogic philosophy. *Light on Yoga, Light on Pranayama, Light on the Yoga Sutras of Patanjali* and *Light on Life* are a few of the many books he has written. Iyengar yoga centers are found all over the world, and millions practice Iyengar yoga. Iyengar's family was poor. He faced numerous challenges and illnesses as a young boy. As a teen he went to live with his brother-in-law, T. Krishnamacharya, and began practicing yoga. His health improved dramatically. Iyengar went on to create a system of yoga, which focuses on strict alignment. Iyengar's own experiences through times of illness inspired him to create aids for the practice of yoga postures. Yoga "props" such as blocks, wedges, and straps can be attributed to B.K.S. Iyengar. In 2004 he was named by *Time Magazine* as one of the one hundred most influential people in the world.

B.K.S. Iyengar left his earthly body on August 20th, 2014. His light will be missed.

The 1930s and 1940s

1945   The birth of A.G. Mohan, a eighteen year student of Krisnamacharya who currently shares his knowledge, wisdom, sense of humor, and gratitude for his teachings through his travels and through the Krishnamacharya Yoga Mandiram in Chennai, India, which he cofounded with his wife, Indra.

Indra Mohan also studied extensively under the tutelage of Krisnamacharya and has coauthored numerous texts with her husband. She is known for her wise, gentle, serene, and compassionate nature.

A.G. and Indra Mohan also cofounded Svastha Yoga and Ayurveda and are joined by their children, Ganesh and Nitya to share the integrated approach to using Ayurveda and Yoga in order to create complete health and balance (Svastha). You may find more information on the Mohans from www.svastha.net.

- Americans began traveling to India to learn Yoga, and Indians begin traveling West to teach. A number of articles on Yoga were published in *Sports Illustrated*.

The 1950s and 1960s

- Swami Sivananda sent Swami Vishnu-Devananda to the West in 1957. Later, Swami Vishnu Devananda established the International Yoga Vedanta Centers.

- In 1967 the Beatles began studying Transcendental Meditation (TM) with Maharishi Mahesh Yogi. In early 1968, the group traveled to Rishikesh, India, to dedicate themselves to his teaching. It is widely believed that the Maharishi's teachings provided a grounding force for band members during an extremely tumultuous time in their careers. In addition, Indian culture is undeniably infused into the band's music after this time. These experiences from India, and the methodology of Transcendental Meditation, inspired them profoundly in their ability to write and record the songs on the *White Album* (http://www.nytimes.com/2008/02/07/arts/music/07yogi.html?scp=3&sq=maha rishi&st=nyt).

- On August 15, 1969, Swami Satchidananda opened the Woodstock Festival in Bethel, New York. The following is a portion of the speech through which he addressed the crowd of approximately 500,000:

My Beloved Brothers and Sisters:

I am overwhelmed with joy to see the entire youth of America gathered here in the name of the fine art of music. In fact, through the music, we can work wonders. Music is a celestial sound and it is the sound that controls the whole universe, not atomic vibrations. Sound energy, sound power, is much, much greater than any other power in this world. And, one thing I would very much wish you all to remember is that with sound, we can make—and at the same time, break. Even in the war-field, to make the tender heart an animal, sound is used. Without that war band, that terrific sound, man will not become animal to kill his own brethren. So, that proves that you can break with sound, and if we care, we can make also.

America leads the whole world in several ways. Very recently, when I was in the East, the grandson of Mahatma Gandhi met me and asked me what's happening in America. and I said, "America is becoming a whole. America is helping everybody in the material field, but the time has come for America to help the whole world with spirituality also." And, that's why from the length and breadth, we see people—thousands of people, yoga-minded, spiritual-minded.

So, let all our actions, and all our arts, express Yoga. Through that sacred art of music, let us find peace that will pervade all over the globe. Often we hear groups of people shouting, "Fight for Peace." I still don't understand how they are going to fight and then find peace. Therefore, let us not fight for peace, but let us find peace within ourselves first.

Before concluding his speech, Satchidananda invited the crowd to join with him "whole-heartedly" in chanting sacred Sanskrit words. The crowd was asked to then participate in one minute of silence (with no cameras clicking) to feel what he called "the great, great power of that sound and the wonderful peace that it can bring in you and into the whole world".

The 1970s to the present

Due to the proliferation of teachers and methods from the 1970s on, an attempt to list and explain them all may be a decade's worth of work.

Present-Day Influential Teachers

Below is a list of some of the most influential Yoga teachers and/or practitioners, not mentioned in the sections above.

Baron Baptiste	Dr. John Kabat-Zinn	A.G.Mohan
Beryl Bender-Birch	Gary Kraftsow	Indra Mohan
Steven Cope	Dr. Judith Hanson Lasater	Dr. Dean Ornish
Mary Dunn		Dr. Mehmet Oz
Maty Ezraty	David Life	Sharath Rangaswami
Lilias Folan	Kino Macgregor	Shiva Rea
Georg Feuerstein	Dr. Timothy McCall	Erich Schiffmann
David Frawley		John Schumacher
Richard Freeman	Tim Miller	David Swenson
Sharon Gannon	Chuck Miller	Patricia Waldon
Richard Hittleman	Sri Dharma Mittra	Rodney Yee

Most qualified instructors have trained extensively in the tradition in which they teach, which requires decades of commitment. Among the thousands of active yoga teachers in the United States today, very few have been granted acharya (master teacher) status from the gurus from whom they learned.

Yoga Alliance—the nonprofit organization for the education and support of yoga in the United States—was created to "ensure that there is a thorough understanding of the benefits of yoga, that the teachers of yoga value its history and traditions, and that the public can be confident of the quality and consistency of instruction" (mission statement from Yoga Alliance, **http://www.yogaalliance.org**).

There is also an International contingent: Yoga Alliance International, the International Association of Yoga Therapists, or IAYT, and the International Yoga Federation, to name a few.

 The Cult Question

A number of people and organizations over the years have attempted to grant cult status to Yoga in general and to numerous systems of Hatha yoga. Some teachers and methods no doubt have been controversial. An underlying misunderstanding often propels these fears, which should be examined more closely.

To help you determine whether a particular method or teacher of yoga is right for you, ask yourself the following questions:

1. Is the teacher of this method teaching primarily for personal gain or in the spirit of helping others?

2. Has this teacher accumulated a great deal of personal financial and material wealth?

3. Is this teacher's method consistent with a yogic path? In other words, does this teacher and method offer a means to better yourself through the eight-limbed path of yoga?

4. Does the teacher just teach yoga postures without regard to the breath or other aspects of yoga?

5. If you ask a teacher, "How long have you been practicing yoga?" and the response is any of the ones listed below, you may want to keep searching.

~ "I do yoga on Thursdays."
~ "I just got certified last weekend."
~ "I started a couple of years ago."
~ "I am reading some books about it."

There are, of course, rare exceptions.

The Ancient Texts of Yoga

The *Vedas*

The *Vedas* are sacred scriptures that are the basis of modern-day Hinduism. People living during the Vedic period relied on rishis, or devoted yogis, to teach them how to live in divine accord with nature.

The *Upanishads*

This ancient text helps to advance and clarify the *Vedas*. The *Upanishads* are a deeply spiritual work, revealing insight on how to follow the spiritual path.

The *Bhagavad Gita*

This enduring classic, most likely written around the second to fifth century BCE and later placed in the epic, *Mahabarata*, builds on, and incorporates, the doctrines found in the *Upanishads*, and is the oldest known documentation devoted completely to Yoga. In the *Gita*, Yoga is described as a means to oppose evil through skillful action, composure under duress, stillness and serenity of the mind, a position of unity, and the capacity to live in a way that is true to our Self.

The *Yoga Sutras*

Written by Patanjali around the second century, BCE, this work is most often referred to as the eight-limbed path of Classical Yoga, or Ashtanga Yoga, and is offered as a source of guidance for the practitioner to reach his or her full potential. The "limbs" will be explored in Chapter 5.

The *Hatha Yoga Pradipika*

Written by Swami Svatmarama in the fifteenth century CE, this text is comprised of four chapters. The *Pradipika* includes information on the postures and breathing techniques, as well as information on the energy pathways, the energy centers, the purifying techniques, and the hand positions of Hatha Yoga. The *Pradipika*, as is the case with all ancient writings, has been translated numerous times by many scholars. From the beginning of Yoga's recorded history, it has been expressed through Sanskrit, a remarkably beautiful language. Translation, unfortunately, has been difficult because some Sanskrit words have no English equivalents.

The Four Main Paths of Yoga

1. ***Bhakti Yoga*** is the yoga of devotion and chanting, which began about four thousand years ago. Considered to be the yoga of the heart, students on this path endeavor to see the Divine in all things.

2. **Karma Yoga** is the yoga of selfless service. Desmond Tutu, Thich Nhat Hanh, Mother Teresa, and Mohandas Gandhi are among those who currently exemplify, or in their lifetime epitomized, this practice.

3. **Jnana Yoga** is the study of the philosophy of Yoga through contemplation, self-study, study of the ancient texts, and meditation.

4. **Raja Yoga** is expressed as Ashtanga Yoga, or the "royal" eight-limbed path, the goal of which is to lead ultimately to samadhi (bliss).

What Is Hatha Yoga?

What most people in the West think of as Yoga is really the practice of Hatha yoga. *Hatha* is a Sanskrit word meaning sun (ha), moon (tha). The word *Hatha* also implies forceful; it is the physical practice of yoga. The purpose of Hatha yoga is to bring balance and harmony to the body and mind in order to prepare the body for stillness and meditation. According to the *Hatha Yoga Pradipika* (2002), Hatha yoga is intended to be a pathway leading to Raja Yoga, and the practitioner cannot expect to experience success in one without the other. While the goal of Hatha yoga is not purely physical fitness, the physical benefits are undeniable. Purification of the body and mind is achieved in Hatha yoga through postures (asanas), purifying practices (kriyas), finger and hand positions (mudras), muscle locks (bandhas), and breathing exercises (pranayama). The *Pradipika* explains these as a means to awaken subtle energy (kundalini) and purify energy pathways (nadis). As energy (prana) moves through the main channel (sushumna nadi), and through the chakras (energy centers), the practitioner can advance through Raja Yoga into a state of consciousness in which the Self (atman) and the mind (citta) become one (cit). This state of consciousness is known as samadhi.

As stated earlier, the main purpose of this text will be for you to learn a short version of the Primary Series of modern-day Ashtanga yoga, one of the systems of hatha yoga. Pattabhi Jois called this practice Ashtanga yoga, with the belief that *all* yoga methods should follow the eight-limbed path (Ashtanga Yoga) as set forth in the *Yoga Sutras*. This has been somewhat confusing to many people and warrants clarification. Jois's Ashtanga yoga system is incredibly physical and athletic. Without the other aspects, or limbs, of yoga philosophy to guide you, it would just look like exercise. Very strenuous exercise at that! At the completion of the semester, you will have something you can use for the rest of your life: a path to wellness for you to follow if you so choose.

Test Your Knowledge

Name _____ **Date** _____

1. What is the definition of Yoga?

2. What are the four main paths of Yoga? Briefly describe each.

3. What are the five main ancient texts of Yoga?

4. What is the definition and the purpose of Hatha yoga?

5. What are the eight limbs of Ashtanga yoga, as presented by Patanjali in the *Yoga Sutras*?

6. Who created modern-day ashtanga vinyasa yoga?

For a list of alphabetized Sanskrit terms, go to http://www.yogajournal.com/article/
beginners/200-key-sanskrit-yoga-terms/

Yoga in the Contemporary World

Courtesy of Alison Donley

"The search may begin with a restless feeling, as if one were being watched. One turns in all directions and sees nothing. Yet one senses that there is a source for this deep restlessness; and the path that leads there is not a path to a strange place, but the path home. ('But you *are* home,' cries the Witch of the North. 'All you have to do is wake up!')"

The journey is hard, for the secret place *where we have always been* is overgrown with thorns and thickets of 'ideas,' of fears and defenses, prejudices and repressions. The Holy Grail is what Zen Buddhists call our own "true nature"; each man is his own savior after all."

—Peter Matthiessen, *The Snow Leopard*

Why Is Yoga So Popular Now?

That question can really be answered in one word: *stress*.

It is reasonable to estimate that there are now twenty-plus million people practicing Hatha yoga in the United States. Why has it become so popular? The short answer to the question is that we *really* need it. We are living way too fast.

Many scientists have estimated that we human beings think upward of sixty thousand thoughts a day. It is also widely believed that the number of thoughts we think per day has increased profoundly in the last hundred years. This is not at all hard to imagine, considering the world in which we now live.

While advancements in technology have made our lives somewhat easier, many have made our lives busier. We are a distracted bunch. Look around. You will see people racing to school or work in the morning with one hand on the steering wheel and one hand holding the coffee (which, apparently, "America runs on") or talking on a cell phone. People text while driving; check social networking sites during "work" time; listen to music while completing tasks, etc. We have televisions and computers with spilt screens and countless applications for our hand-held devices. Knowing how these things affect our ability to concentrate, it is hard to understand how or why so many people tolerate this behavior.

The Internet is having a profound effect on the way we think. That is the subject of "The Shallows" an investigation by Nicholas Carr into the way technology shapes the way we think. He discusses the effects of specific inventions such as the typewriter, the printing press, and the computer. Technological advances are occurring at an ever accelerating pace and our minds are adapting to keep up. There was a time when even on a computer, you could only do one thing at a time. This is obviously no longer the case. Among today's youth, even the inherently chaotic nature of video games is not enough to satiate the need for multiple, fast moving stimuli. Gamers now talk to opponents while texting and web surfing.

According to Carr, to adapt to our changing technological landscape the way the brain works is changing, quite literally. Neural pathways are rerouted to process information according to the way it is received. Instead of the deep, retrospective thinking that a good book might initiate, when "surfing the net" the brain is exposed to vast variety of information, often at a superficial level, very quickly, thus negatively impacting our ability to focus and obviating the need to remember, because we can just look it up again.

Societal pressures have helped to create the illusion that multitasking is somehow not only acceptable but also actually helpful in our high-tech world. Some smartphones are marketed as superior because they allow us to do a number of things while on the go. While this may be a selling point as far as the corporations go, it is (to say the least) a scary proposition.

Numerous studies have been done to determine the value of multitasking. In a 2009 study, a group of Stanford researchers found that multitasking actually impairs cognitive control. They found that people who are repeatedly flooded with a number of sources of electronic information are not able to pay attention, control memory, or go from one task to another as efficiently or effectively as those who chose to complete one thing at a time. Furthermore, research has shown, with rare exception, multitasking creates a temporary drop in IQ and takes a toll on our mental energy, especially when the tasks are more complex.

Multitaskers are "suckers for irrelevancy," says communications Professor Clifford Nass, one of the researchers whose findings appeared in the August 24 edition of the *Proceedings of the National Academy of Sciences*. "Everything distracts them (**http://news.stanford.edu/news/2009/ august24/multitask-research-study-082409.html**)."

Social scientists have long assumed that it's impossible to process more than one string of information at a time. The brain just can't do it. But many researchers conjecture that people who appear to multitask must have superb control over what they think about and what they pay attention to.

Through a series of experiments, the researchers at Stanford attempted to determine what "gift," if any, the high multitaskers had over the low multitaskers for storing and organizing information; for memorization, and for switching from one task to another. In all tests the low multitaskers outperformed the heavy multitaskers. It seems that the brain is slowed down by information irrelevant to the task at hand. Researchers are currently studying chronic media multitaskers to determine if they are born with an inability to concentrate, or if they are impairing their cognitive control through their repeated actions (**http://news.stanford.edu/news/2009/ august24/multitask-research-study-082409.html**).

Will our brains adapt through the years, making multitasking a necessity? That question may be answered many decades from now; however, leading social scientists are giving the "thumbs down." Our brains are just not wired for it.

For now it seems that less really *is* more.

 ## What *Are* Our Brains Wired for?

In the last twenty-five years, a great deal has been discovered about how the human brain works. It is exciting to imagine what the next twenty-five years will tell us. What we do know now, from the research being done in medicine and neuroscience, is that the brain is hard-wired for certain capabilities. Below are a number of the common abilities of the human brain that affect not just our personal wellness but also the state of the communities in which we live, society in general, and ultimately the state of the world.

Caring for and serving others	Hierarchy
Community	Math
Competition	Music
Connection with others	Spirituality (faith, religion, prayer, meditation)
Cooperation	

> I slept and dreamt that life was joy. I awoke and saw that life was service.
> I acted and behold, service was joy.
>
> —Rabindranath Tagore

David Korten discusses the value of compassion in the July 2008 *Yes!* Magazine article, "We Are Hard Wired to Care and Connect." Korten suggests that survival of the fittest may not be a reference to greed and competition, as we have been taught, but, instead, that the unselfish delivery of compassion will be the quality that guarantees not only the survival of the individual but the entire human race. According to Korten, the unquestioned pillars of our society will not only lead to our downfall but are, quite simply, unnatural. "We humans are born to connect, learn, and serve and that it is indeed within our means to create family-friendly communities in which we get our satisfaction from caring relationships rather than material consumption."

Studies reveal that human emotions mirror the physiological effects of eustress and distress. Helping others improves the immune system, lowers heart rate, and triggers an "approach and soothe" reaction. Korten's article emphasizes what should be obvious: If we weren't wired for helping others and acting on behalf of the communities in which we live, we likely wouldn't even be around to have the conversation (**http://www.yesmagazine.org/issues/purple-america/ we-are-hard-wired-to-care-and-connect**).

 ## Your Brain on Yoga

Neurons, the building blocks of your brain, communicate through electrical changes, or brain waves, which can be seen in an electroencephalogram, or EEG. Brain waves are typically categorized (for convenience) into four main groups (bulleted) and two subdivisions (*asterisk),

depending on frequency, or hertz (Hz). Hertz is measured by the number of cycles per second and is determined by neural activity (**http://www.brainandhealth.com/Brain-Waves.html**).

- **Delta waves** (below 4 Hz) happen during sleep.

- **Theta waves** (4 to 7 Hz) occur during sleep, deep relaxation (like hypnotic relaxation), and visualization. These patterns are typical in yoga nidra (yogic "sleep") and deep states of meditation.

- **Alpha waves** (8 to 13 Hz) are created when we are calm and relaxed, as in a gentle yoga asana practice, or a highly refined vigorous asana practice.

  *SMR or sensory motor rhythm (around 14 Hz) links brain and body functions.

- **Beta waves** (13 to 38 Hz) are involved during problem solving and active thinking. If the brain remains in this pattern for long periods, the hormones necessary for increased energy (adrenaline and cortisol) can create mental and physical fatigue and, quite possibly, a brain that is producing no new neurons.

- **Gamma brain waves** (39 to 100 Hz) occur during periods of higher mental activity and information consolidation. Before and during meditation, Tibetan monks were shown to have elevated levels of gamma waves as compared to nonmeditators in a recent study.

In an article focusing on brain function and the production of gamma waves, "Meditation Gives Brain a Charge, Study Finds" by Marc Kauffman (*Washington Post*, January 3, 2005), Richard Davidson discusses his findings.

"What we found is that the longtime practitioners showed brain activation on a scale we have never seen before," said Davidson, a neuroscientist at the new ten-million-dollar University of Wisconsin–Madison's W. M. Keck Laboratory for Functional Brain Imaging and Behavior.

Davidson collaborated with Tibet's Dalai Lama, the face of Buddhism in today's world, to study yoga's impact on the brain. The evidence from the study shows unequivocally that meditation, in this case, on the concept of unconditional compassion ("unrestricted readiness and availability to help living beings"), actually changed the structure of the brain to produce extremely high levels of the desirable gamma waves.

In an article titled "The Scientific Basis for Yoga Therapy," Timothy McCall, MD, discusses research to support and explain the benefits of yoga that yoga practitioners have known intuitively for centuries. The very title of the article with its reference to "yoga therapy" speaks to the legitimization of yoga in Western medical circles. Medicine and science in the West are investigating all areas of Eastern holistic health practices and techniques. Dr. McCall published the book, *Yoga As Medicine: The Yogic Prescription for Health and Healing* in 2010. You will find Dr. McCall's Yoga as Medicine "75 Conditions Benefited by Yoga (as shown in scientific studies) on his website www.drmccall.com

In just the last few years, research has documented the efficacy of yoga for such conditions as back pain, multiple sclerosis, insomnia, cancer, heart disease, and even tuberculosis. Studies are also increasingly documenting how yoga works. Among its many beneficial effects, yoga has been shown to increase strength, flexibility, and balance; enhance immune function; lower blood sugar and cholesterol levels; and improve psychological well-being. One of yoga's most prominent effects, of course, is stress reduction (**http://www.yogajournal.com/for_teachers/2016**).

Dr. McCall notes that current brain structure concepts indicate that the brain is constantly rewiring itself based on repeated thought patterns. This process is called neuroplasticity. The more repetition, the stronger the new neural pathways become. Obviously, if the thoughts are negative, unhealthy behaviors can become the norm. On the other hand, if the brain is processing positive messages, dramatic changes for the better can result. Devoted yoga practice can have a profound impact on behavior. Dr. McCall states that "The resulting neural networks—or samskaras, as yogis call them—get stronger and stronger as you stay with the practice. Slowly but surely, these healthy grooves of thought and action help guide people out of the ruts in which they've been stuck." In addition, simply the fact that yoga improves body awareness motivates practitioners to stop behaviors that make them feel bad (**http://www.yogajournal.com/for_teachers/2016**).

Overall, brain activity is a blend of frequencies—some stronger and in greater quantities than others—depending on thoughts and actions. Different states of consciousness are generated by different patterns and types of brain wave frequencies. In order to function optimally, the brain really needs to be resilient. It needs to be able to shift into another gear when something is not working well. Difficulty arises when we cannot alter our brain activity to meet the demands of life and when we get "stuck" in a certain pattern.

This inability of the brain to bounce back ("stuck-ness") can come from a number of things: stress, injury, physical pain, emotional pain, medication(s), drug and alcohol consumption, and fatigue. A person whose brain gets stuck in a slower pattern will have many difficulties, such as lack of concentration, focus, and clarity of thought.

Stress: The Basics

***Stress* is the physiological reaction to a stressor: anything new, frightening, threatening or exciting.**

A *stressor* is the stress causing agent or event.

In addition to the daily stress from being a living, breathing human being, most of us experience a daily bombardment from family, school or workplace, and the community and society in which we live. Most professional and academic institutions recognize the following types of stress:

Hypostress is a result of having too little to do. Restlessness, constant boredom, and a lack of inspiration are "lowmarks" of hypostress.

Hyperstress is the extreme opposite of hypostress. Hyperstress is the consequence of having too much pressure and being constantly overstimulated and overscheduled. Working in a fast-paced job, or struggling to balance the pressure of work and family, can create hyperstress.

Eustress is a short-term stress created from a positive event. It enhances creativity, gives us strength, enthusiasm, and inspiration.

Distress can be either acute or chronic. It is negative or harmful stress that can cause harm to the body and mind. Distress often is caused by too much responsibility, too much work, financial problems, relationship issues, insomnia, chronic illness, and loss.

Our bodies are well equipped to handle stress in small bursts. The autonomic nervous system kicks into gear to bail us out in tough situations by triggering the **stress response.**

The stressresponse is activated when the brain perceives an impending stressor, especially one we may feel ill-equipped to handle, and sends us into "fight or flight," which is our sympathetic nervous system response to the situation.

The diagram below represents the stress response:

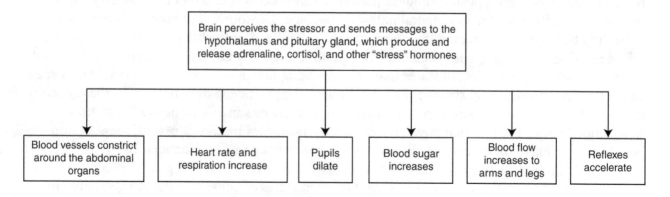

If and when the situation is resolved, the parasympathetic response, or "rest and digest," takes over and the following is observed:

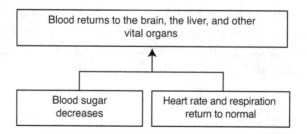

Stress can have wide-ranging effects on emotions, mood, and behavior. Equally important, but often less appreciated, are effects on various systems, organs, and tissues all over the body.

 How Does a Yoga Asana Practice Help?

Your asana practice becomes a beautiful island sanctuary in this sea of sensory overstimulation in which most of us swim. We can all find solace in reducing our multitasked lives to a practice of simplicity and self-awareness. Rather than focusing on numerous things within any given minute, during a practice session we are tuning in to three things: breath, muscle locks, and focus points. If we allow these three things to guide our movement, all extraneous things fall away. We are then able to truly experience what we are seeing or feeling with clarity and presence.

The cultivation of this moving meditation will begin to translate to the outside world. You will likely find yourself stepping off the mat at the end of practice, able to carry the "vibe" you have created with you for the rest of the day. With continued practice, you will find yourself using breath in all kinds of situations to pull yourself from frenetic energy into a calm state of presence.

Instead of thinking or saying things like "I am stressed out!" you will have the wisdom to recognize that *you* are not stressed out, but you *are* allowing a stressor or stressors (they don't typically come one at a time) to affect you physiologically. A more accurate assessment of a stressful situation will be possible when we acknowledge and accept that our response to most stressors is a personal choice we are making. This is a hefty responsibility. There will be no one else to blame.

Let's say you end up in a heated conversation, and anger is surfacing on both sides. Rather than letting the other person know how angry you are, can you just observe the anger? Can you observe the tension in the neck, shoulders, and face? Can you observe the breath becoming shallow?

Do you have the patience to breathe your way to a state of calm? Can you just *listen* in a relaxed state of awareness to what the other person is saying before peacefully responding to what has been said?

An asana practice will teach you those skills, because you have to do *all* of those things: loving and patient observation of a posture, breath control, careful adjustment or response to what is needed, etc. This will be profoundly empowering.

Your yoga primer for the semester to follow will be a work in progress. It will most likely take a while to slow the racing, multitasking mind down. Upon recognizing when the mind is racing, you have already mastered the awareness that the mind *is* indeed racing. A remarkable first step in the process! Now, what can be done to slow it down? Breathe. Examine the breath. What is the quality of the breath? Is it strained or jagged? Develop and nurture a breath with a silky smooth texture and a deep, steady quality. Observe how the mind begins to slow down. In time, during your asana practice, this beautiful breath (along with awareness of particular focal points and specific muscle locks) allows the mind to become so steady, focused, and clear that all unnecessary sensory stimulation will fall away.

You will have days when you feel light as a feather with energy to spare. In contrast, you will have days when your body feels like wet cement and your brain feels foggy. Honor your Self by listening to your body with love and compassion. Give it exactly what it needs on any given day. Meet your energy exactly where it is and start from there. As Einstein said, "nothing happens until something moves."

People come to yoga for many reasons. Some come for functional reasons: to swing a golf club more efficiently, to go on weekend adventures without injury, to improve flexibility for a competitive sport, to lose weight for health reasons, to create a respite from grief, depression, anxiety, etc. Some come for egotistic reasons: to look better, to improve muscle tone, or (as a current DVD on the market states) to get a "Yoga Butt." No matter the reason, most find not only results but also solace as well from the practice, *even* if they came just for the sculpted buttocks!

Popular Styles of Hatha Yoga

There are many styles of yoga. The differences in these styles usually are on what the main focus of the practice should be. Some styles require vinyasa, which is the linking of movement with breath, while others emphasize the movement of energy through breath work or strict alignment of the body. All styles share common roots. Not one style can rightfully claim that it is better than other styles—we are all individuals, and what feels right to one person may not be at all comfortable to another. It is a matter of personal preference.

Following are brief descriptions of many styles of Hatha yoga, all of which could be considered modern yoga, having evolved within the last two hundred years from the many schools, or traditions, of Yoga.

Ananda Ananda yoga is a classical style of Hatha yoga that uses asana and pranayama to awaken, experience, and begin to control the subtle energies within yourself, especially the energies of the chakras. Its object is to use those energies to harmonize body, mind, and emotions, and above all to attune yourself with higher levels of awareness. One unique feature of this system is the use of silent affirmations while in the asanas as a means of working more directly and consciously with the subtle energies to achieve this attunement. Ananda yoga is a relatively gentle, inward experience, not an athletic or aerobic practice. It was developed by Swami Kriyananda, a direct disciple of Paramhansa Yogananda, author of the spiritual classic, *Autobiography of a Yogi.*

Ashtanga For those who want a serious workout, Ashtanga may be the perfect yoga. Developed by Sri K. Pattabhi Jois, Ashtanga is physically demanding. Participants move through a series of flows, jumping from one posture to another to build strength, flexibility, and stamina. It is not for beginners or anyone who has been taking a leisurely approach to fitness. The so-called *power yoga* is based on Ashtanga.

Integral Developed by Swami Satchidananda, the man who taught the crowds at the original Woodstock to chant "Om," Integral classes put almost as much emphasis on pranayama and meditation as they do on postures. Integral yoga is used by Dr. Dean Ornish in his ground-breaking work on reversing heart disease, titled, *Dr. Dean Ornish's Program for Reversing Heart Disease*.

Iyengar Ever think standing was just a matter of keeping your body on top of your legs? It's hard to appreciate how involved a simple thing like just standing can be, how much concentration and how many subtle movements and adjustments it takes, until you take an Iyengar yoga class. Of course, the point is that you are not *just* standing. You're doing Tadasana, Mountain Pose, and in yoga in the style of B.K.S. Iyengar, Tadasana is an active pose. B.K.S. Iyengar is one of the best-known yoga teachers and the creator of one of the most popular styles of yoga in the world. His style of yoga is noted for great attention to detail and the precise alignment of postures, as well as the use of props such as blocks and belts. No doubt part of Iyengar's success is due to the quality of teachers, who must complete a rigorous two- to five-year training program for certification.

Kripalu Called the yoga of consciousness, Kripalu puts great emphasis on proper breath, alignment, coordinating breath and movement, and "honoring the wisdom of the body." You work according to the limits of your individual flexibility and strength. Alignment follows awareness. Students learn to focus on the physical and psychological reactions caused by various postures to develop their awareness of mind, body, emotion, and spirit. There are three stages in Kripalu yoga. Stage One focuses on learning the postures and exploring your body's abilities. Stage Two involves holding the postures for an extended time, developing concentration and inner awareness. Stage Three is like a meditation in motion, in which the movement from one posture to another arises unconsciously and spontaneously.

Kundalini Kundalini yoga in the tradition of Yogi Bhajan, who brought the style to the West in 1969, focuses on the controlled release of Kundalini energy. The practice involves classic poses, breath, coordination of breath and movement, and meditation.

Sivananda Sivananda is one of the world's largest schools of yoga. Developed by Vishnu-devananda and named for his teacher, Sivananda yoga follows a set structure that includes pranayama, classic asanas, and relaxation. Vishnu-devananda wrote one of the contemporary yoga classics, *The Complete Illustrated Book of Yoga*. First published in 1960, the book is still one of the best introductions to yoga available.

Svaroopa Developed by Rama Berch, Svaroopa yoga teaches significantly different ways of doing familiar poses, emphasizing the opening of the spine by beginning at the tailbone and progressing in turn through each spinal area. Every pose integrates the foundational principles of asana, anatomy and yoga philosophy, and emphasizes the development of transcendent inner experience, which is called svaroopa by Patanjali in the *Yoga Sutras*. This is a consciousness-oriented yoga that also promotes healing and transformation. Svaroopa is not an athletic endeavor but a development of consciousness using the body as a tool.

Viniyoga Viniyoga is not so much a style as it is a methodology for developing practices for individual conditions and purposes. This is the approach developed by Sri. T. Krishnamacharya, teacher of well-known contemporary masters B.K.S. Iyengar, K. Pattabhi Jois, A.G. Indra Devi and Indra Mohan, and continued by his son, T.K.V. Desikachar. Key characteristic of the asana practice are the careful integration of the flow of breath with movement of the spine—with sequencing, adaptations and intensity dependent upon the overall context and goals. Function is stressed over form. Practices may also include pranayama, meditation, reflection, study, and other classic elements. Personal practices are taught privately. Given the scope of practice, the inherent therapeutic applications and the heritage of the lineage, the training requirements for teacher certification are extensive.

Many additional styles of Hatha yoga have evolved from a number of early traditional systems. Newer styles of Hatha yoga may represent a particular system, or may be an offshoot of an earlier method. It is important to know that yoga was intended to be for everyone. The numerous styles represent an understanding of what was passed down from teacher to student. Traditionally, a guru passed his knowledge on to a student, who, after many decades of practice, would then become a teacher. Many believe that it is essential to have a guru, while others feel that enlightenment can and will come as a result of following the methodology that best suits the individual. The word *guru* can be translated as someone who brings those who are in darkness into the light.

The traditional model has suffered recently due to the proliferation of yoga schools and training programs. Most students—through reverence to the lineage from which they learned—choose to stay true to that lineage. Others may choose to introduce their own knowledge, life experience, and creativity to form an offshoot of the original teaching.

Yoga was not intended to be a product. However, in many countries, yoga undeniably has become just that. A quick online search can reveal clothing for yoga practice, as well as mats, props, water bottles, jewelry, bags, headbands, DVDs, practice cards, posters, etc. One teacher in particular has extracted postures and placed them in a sequence which he then had copyrighted. As a result, anyone wishing to teach "his" yoga must be licensed and certified to do so. This "yogi" then sued any studio who taught his methodology if they have not taken the proper steps and paid the required fee. While this approach is *clearly not* at all yogic, and has recently been overturned in court, it has created an enormous interest for thousands of people who attend studios to learn this particular method.

There are two additional styles of yoga worthy of mention:

Restorative Yoga Restorative yoga has grown in popularity in large part, due to the efforts of Judith Hanson Lasater, Ph.D., PT, and senior Iyengar yoga teacher (**http://www. restorativeyogateachers.com/**). This style of yoga offers a variety of asanas that are done with the support of various props, such as blankets and bolsters. This yoga style is perfect for people who are in need of the gentle, tender loving care this practice offers.

Laughter Yoga Developed by Indian guru Jiten Kohi and made popular by Dr. Madan Kataria, this form of yoga employs self-initiated laughter and specialized yoga breathing techniques. These bouts of laughter do not necessarily involve humor or comedy. The "fake" laughter soon turns into real laughter because, as we all know, laughter truly is contagious. In a Laughter yoga class, one person may initiate a hearty (albeit fake) laugh, and within seconds, the rest of the group is laughing. Much has been written about the medicinal value of laughter, and research has proven that laughter does much to reduce stress and create healing energy in the body (*Anatomy of an Illness*, 1979). To learn more about Laughter yoga, please see Mary Desmond Pinkowish's article in the in the August 2009 issue of *ODE* magazine titled *"Medicinal Mirth: The Health Benefits of Laughter"* at **http://www.odemagazine.com/doc/65/medicine-of-mirth**.

There *are* yoga classes to steer clear of:

Joe yoga and *Jane yoga*

Okay, so those are made up....

However, note that weekend "certifications" exist for anyone desiring to become a yoga teacher. Yes, this means that an individual knowing absolutely *nothing* about yoga can go to a single (one!) weekend of training and leave with a piece of paper stating that he or she is a certified yoga teacher. This is not only absurd but frightening as well. Perhaps this is why the recent statistics for yoga-related injuries have risen so dramatically. This is an unfortunate result of the radical proliferation of teachers offering a system of self-care that was intended to promote health and wellness. For most seasoned yoga teachers, it is unfathomable to imagine attempting to teach yoga without prior decades of practice and study.

Test Your Knowledge

Name _____ **Date** _____

1. Summarize, in at least one paragraph, why Hatha yoga has become so popular in the last twenty years.

2. List five things our brain is hard-wired for.

3. Please define:

   - Stress

   - Hypostress

   - Eustress

   - Hyperstress

   - Distress

4. Name two styles of Hatha yoga listed in Chapter 2 that appeal to you. What interests you about those styles?

5. What does the word *vinyasa* mean?

6. How does a yoga practice help to reduce stress? At least two paragraphs please.

Going Deeper: "OMwork"

Choose one day this week (in advance) to:

- Turn off your TV and/or any other "weapon of mass distraction" (WMD). Use your computer only for work, and try to limit the time to exactly what you need to complete the work assignment. Journal your experience.

- Turn off your cell phone. If necessary, let friends and family know ahead of time that for this one day they should call or text you *only if it is a true emergency*. Turn it on only twice on this day to check, but do not place any calls or write any texts. Journal your experience.

For three days in a row this week, immediately upon rising from the night's sleep, sit at the edge of the bed and set an intention for the day. Sit and take ten to twenty deep breaths before standing and going about your day. Journal your experience.

Choose one-half day this week to refrain from speaking unless you must for work, school, or safety reasons. If necessary, let friends and family members know ahead of time. Journal your experience.

Watch a comedy. ☺

Links to sites with additional information on the effects of stress include:

- www.drmccall.com
- www.nimh.nih.gov—National Institute of Mental Health
- www.nmha.org—National Mental Health Association
- www.mentalhealth.com—*Encyclopedia of Mental Health* information

Wellness

Health is a state of complete harmony of the body, mind and spirit. When one is free from physical disabilities and mental distractions, the gates of the soul open.

—B.K.S. Iyengar

In *Fitness and Wellness*, a textbook by W. K. Hoeger and S. A. Hoeger (2007), the term *wellness* is defined as the constant and deliberate effort to stay healthy and achieve the highest potential for well-being. Of the many definitions for wellness that are available, this one stands out. The phrase "constant and deliberate effort" implies that making wise choices can have a profound effect on our lives, given the myriad choices we are faced with every day.

 ## The Seven Dimensions of Wellness

According to the National Wellness Institute, the National Institutes of Health, and many other health promotion agencies, wellness is multidimensional. Numerous universities, corporations, and health programs pursue the following model of wellness, which encompasses seven dimensions:

Social   Physical

Occupational   Intellectual

Environmental   Emotional/Mental

Spiritual

 ## Wellness Questions

Please answer the following questions regarding the seven dimensions of wellness. Each of these dimensions is represented with three to five questions. Record your answers directly or use separate paper. Elaborate on the answers as you wish. You will be the only one (if you choose) who will see your answers:

1. Do you have a good social network?

2. Do you feel a part of your community?

3. Do you feel supported (emotionally) by your friends?

4. Do you feel supported (emotionally) by your family?

5. Are your personal relationships healthy ones?

6. Do you have a job? (If no, skip #7.)

7. Do you feel safe at your job?

8. Do you feel confident in your ability to secure a job in your field of study after graduation?

9. Do you feel your choice of vocation will suit your desired lifestyle?

10. Do you feel confident in your job skills?

11. Do you feel that your job (current or desired) is one that will allow you to feel you are making a positive difference in your community or the world?

12. Do you live in a safe area?

13. Are you exposed to dangerous materials where you live or work?

14. Is the air clean where you live or work?

15. Do you have clean water to drink?

16. Do you take care of the environment? Do you reduce, reuse, recycle, and restore?

17. Do you believe in something larger than yourself?

18. Does your religion support you?

19. Do you feel you are a part of the "bigger picture"?

20. Do you feel physically fit? Do you have adequate muscular strength, endurance, and flexibility? Do you have good heart and lung function? Is your body composition (the ratio of lean muscle and adipose or fat tissue) healthy?

21. Are you satisfied with your appearance?

22. What activities do you participate in for fitness?

23. Do you feel hindered by any injuries, disorders, or diseases?

24. Do you feel challenged intellectually?

25. Do you experience work or school settings where you interact with like-minded people?

26. With free time, what topic would you enjoy learning more about?

27. Does your employment satisfy you intellectually? If you are not currently employed, do you feel your future employment will be intellectually fulfilling?

28. Is there any mental illness in your family?

29. Is there any mental illness within your social network?

30. Do you manage your time well? If not, what do you perceive to be the daily time killers that could be better managed?

31. Do you manage your emotions well?

32. What are the most common emotions that you experience on a day-to-day basis? Please circle the ones you experience most frequently from the list provided below.

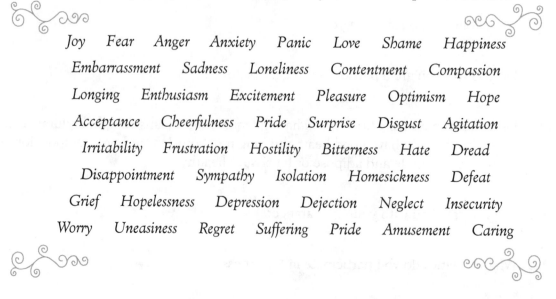

Joy   Fear   Anger   Anxiety   Panic   Love   Shame   Happiness

Embarrassment   Sadness   Loneliness   Contentment   Compassion

Longing   Enthusiasm   Excitement   Pleasure   Optimism   Hope

Acceptance   Cheerfulness   Pride   Surprise   Disgust   Agitation

Irritability   Frustration   Hostility   Bitterness   Hate   Dread

Disappointment   Sympathy   Isolation   Homesickness   Defeat

Grief   Hopelessness   Depression   Dejection   Neglect   Insecurity

Worry   Uneasiness   Regret   Suffering   Pride   Amusement   Caring

33. Please list below the emotions you desire to experience on a daily basis. What do you perceive to be the obstacle blocking your ability to experience these emotions daily?

One of the dimensions of wellness we will explore much more thoroughly through the semester will be the physical dimension.

🪷 Physical Fitness

While there are numerous definitions for "physical fitness," we should keep in mind that any explanation would be incomplete if it did not emphasize the individual's effort to create or maintain the quality of physical fitness. *Physical fitness* can be defined as the general capability to adjust and react positively to physical effort. We need to be physically fit in order to perform daily activities with energy and attentiveness. Basically, we need to be fit enough to go through a day without getting tired. Remember that? How old do you suppose you were when you could get through a *whole* day with energy and then feel sleepy enough to get a really good night's sleep? What was it you did regularly at that age? Why is it that as we age we stop rolling around, running to get from point A to point B, giggling, climbing, jumping, etc.? If we were born with instruction tags, what do you think your tag would say?

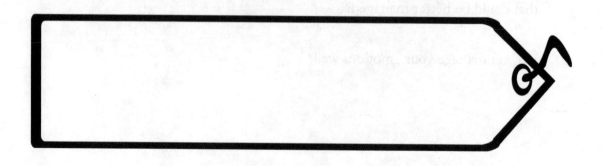

Most academic institutions recognize the health-related components of physical fitness to be muscular strength, muscular flexibility, muscular endurance, cardiorespiratory endurance, and body composition.

- Muscular strength is the ability of a muscle, or group of muscles, to exert force.

- Muscular flexibility is the range of motion around a joint and is measured by the degree of movement around that joint.

- Muscular endurance is the ability of a muscle, or a group of muscles, to perform repeated muscular contractions against resistance for an extended period of time. It is the muscle's ability to continue to perform without fatigue is associated with muscular endurance.

- Body composition is the amount of lean muscle mass and the amount of adipose, or fat tissue, in the body.

- Cardiorespiratory endurance is the strength and endurance of the heart and lungs.

Reaction time, agility, speed, balance, power, coordination, and kinesthetic awareness, or body awareness, are all skill-related components of physical fitness. Skill-related components of fitness are primarily beneficial in athletic endeavors and, for the general population, are not nearly as important as health-related components.

The practice of yoga postures and breath work can greatly enhance all of the health-related components and arguably all but two (reaction time and speed) of the skill-related components. When you begin a yoga practice, your level of fitness, as well as your effort, will determine the degree of improvement experienced throughout the semester. Many of you will be able to feel a difference in body composition over the semester, as well as an improvement in lung capacity.

Additionally, a large number of you will be able to measure an improvement in muscular strength, endurance, and flexibility. Because we will continue to build on to our physical practice with each class, you will be naturally following the training principles of overload and progression. Overload places a load on the body that is greater than it is accustomed to. Progression gradually increases that load over time so the body will adapt and improve. As lung capacity improves, the breath will become longer, allowing you to remain in the postures for lengthier periods of time.

Specificity is another training principle that you should heed regarding athletics. The training must specifically address the elements of fitness you are attempting to improve. For example, if your goal is to improve muscular strength, cardiovascular training is not the most effective means of doing so.

Results of two studies in the September/October 2002 *Yoga Journal* clearly indicate the positive link between yoga and fitness. In "Is Yoga Enough to Keep You Fit?" Alisa Bauman cites studies performed at the University of California at Davis; coauthored by Ezra A. Amsterdam, M.D., as well as the study done by Dee Ann Birkel, an emeritus professor at Ball State's School of Physical Education. Both studies included subjects ranging in fitness levels from smokers to athletes. Each group showed significant improvement in *all* of the components of physical fitness. The benefits for individuals with low fitness levels seem obvious, but the fact that even well-trained athletes were able to increase strength, flexibility, and cardiovascular fitness levels speaks to the power of yoga as a fitness training tool.

Obviously, the individual fitness results achieved through a Hatha yoga practice are commensurate to the effort put forth, as well as the particular style of yoga being practiced. A few styles of Hatha yoga are incredibly physical: Ashtanga is one of the more vigorous. Of course, the more devoted you are to the practice, the more benefits you will enjoy.

Test Your Knowledge

Name _____ **Date** _____

1. What is the definition of wellness?

2. List the seven dimensions of wellness.

3. What does the term "physically fit" imply?

4. What are the health-related components of physical fitness?

5. What are the skill-related components of physical fitness?

6. Summarize in at least two paragraphs, the results of the studies at the University of California at Davis coauthored by Ezra A. Amsterdam, M.D, and Dee Ann Birkel, at Ball State's School of Physical Education.

- Purchase a package of small sticky notes. Write short, positive messages to yourself on a handful of these. These messages should embody the emotions you wish to feel more often. You may select affirmations from the section on samtosa (contentment) in Chapter 5, if you wish. Post these in places you will see throughout the day.

Suggestions for strategic placement:

A bathroom mirror

The refrigerator door

Your alarm clock

A bedside table

The dashboard of your car

Your computer screen

Your wallet

Take a photo of your sticky notes and select as your home screen wallpaper on your cell phone.

The Benefits of Practicing Yoga

 ## Student Testimonials

The following testimonials are from students from Yoga I classes at WCU and students of The Light Within Yoga Studio 2009–2010.

"Yoga this semester has been an amazing experience. It has been a way of life for me throughout these last few months. When I am not practicing the physical aspect of yoga, I am experiencing the mental and emotional aspects. Much of my attitude and outlook on life has improved and I found that my stress has significantly decreased. Severe depression runs in my family and yoga has saved me from that. I will continue to practice yoga for the rest of my life. Why wouldn't I want to continue something that helped me to love myself?"

—Katie Y.

"As an athlete I would have to say yoga was very effective for relieving soreness, and for injury prevention. There is a great amount of time spent training for football and pushing our bodies to extreme limits; the importance of stretching is often forgotten. Yoga enabled me to really spend significant time to restore my body and increase flexibility. That is very important as an athlete."

—Ronnie K.

"At the time that I started yoga three-ish years ago, I was at a very dark place in my life. Personally and emotionally, things were a total mess. Physically, I was trying (without success) to accept a body that had bounced back remarkably from a serious eating disorder that had peaked (or plummeted) with a heart attack two years earlier. As I continue to wrestle with my ambivalent feelings regarding my "new" body, yoga has been an essential element in my struggle to cope with the changes that have occurred. I am now stronger and probably healthier than ever, and I am finally beginning to appreciate this fact for the miracle that it is. My practice has helped me to arrive at mental and emotional states that are much easier to live with on a daily basis. I would suspect that this is a blessing for those around me too!"

—Kate S.

"Yoga practice has helped me control my breathing more effectively during wrestling practice and whenever I work out. It has also made me more flexible and encouraged me to eat healthier and follow a healthier lifestyle."

—Perry D.

"This yoga practice has had a great impact on me. My intention for the practice was to focus on being *here*—not anything that happened earlier or something that needs to be done later. I have been able to carry that intention throughout my day and it has helped with every aspect of my semester."

—Lauren S.

"My yoga practice has taught me a lot of patience. I am slow to anger since I have practiced yoga. Also the breathing has helped me especially when I am in a stressed situation. When I do the breathing it calms me down. Taking yoga this semester has also taught me how to be disciplined. I was never active growing up and this has taught me physical and mental discipline".

—Danielle T.

"Yoga has saved me. Prior to this semester I moved away from my family, left an abusive relationship, and had a traumatic event occur with my body. I have a hard time asking for help. I am an independent woman. Yoga showed me that I am AMAZING. When I step on my mat, the outside world no longer exists—it is only me and my mat. I feel myself and everything worth fighting for. Without yoga, I wouldn't know how to get up in the morning with a smile. Yoga came into my life at a perfect time."

—Kasi C.

"My yoga practice has affected me in many ways this semester. This past cross country season ended up being the best of my running career and I believe that is because I have been able to stay injury free through yoga. I ended up beating my best time by 45 seconds in the 6K. The difference yoga has made in the way my body feels is truly amazing and I plan on continuing to practice through the rest of my life."

—Jess J.

I decided to take yoga as an elective when I was a student at West Chester University. I had such a positive experience that I continue to practice to this day. I had anxiety in the past and was prescribed medication before I was introduced to yoga. While taking medication, I felt that it was only masking my emotions and made me feel numb to my anxiety. I believe anxiety is a symptom when your mind, body, and soul, are not in synchrony. It wasn't until the second semester of my yoga practice that I felt *pure joy* during standing tree pose. I am thankful for my experience because as a person in the counseling profession, yoga continues to help me stay balanced.

—Janice R.

Benefits of Yoga Practice as Reported by Students

We often hear about methods like yoga as "mind, body, spirit" practices. On a purely physical level, hatha yoga works all systems of the body: muscular, skeletal, circulatory, nervous, endocrine, lymphatic, respiratory, urinary, digestive, reproductive and immune. As mentioned earlier, yoga can help a person improve all of the health-related components of physical fitness and many of skill-related components of physical fitness as well. On a mental/emotional level, a yoga practitioner can apply the insights gained from practice to handle daily stress more efficiently and effectively.

Below are some of the many benefits of yoga practice as reported by WCU students through the last twelve years:

Improvement in muscle tone

Improvement in muscular strength

Improvement in muscular endurance

Increased flexibility

Improvement in balance

Increased energy

Spiritual awareness

Improvement in depression-related symptoms

Decreased back pain

Decreased neck pain

Cessation of physical pain that had been chronic

Greater ability to handle emotional pain

Cessation of tooth grinding

Mood improvement

Ability to feel peaceful

Ability to feel content

Improvement in body awareness

Improvement in body image

Improved self esteem

Improved ability to focus

Enhanced creativity

Better sleep

Cessation of insomnia

Improved ability to handle stress

Weight loss

Smoking cessation

Decreased anxiety

A significant decrease in stress related symptoms

Improvement in skin conditions

Improvement in circulation problems

Decrease in blood sugar levels

Improvement in concentration

Improvement in academics

Improvement in relationships

Enhanced athletic performance

Asthma improvement

One of the most rewarding answers recorded on an end-of-semester evaluation to the question, "what did you like best about this class?" was: "I had fun."

As you may have extracted from the testimonials and the student-reported benefits above, yoga can have a profound effect on wellness. Over many years, I have witnessed the overwhelmingly positive results of yoga practice for students with mild to moderate depression, anxiety, and panic disorder. There is an increasing amount of research documenting the psychological value of a yoga practice, and this is precisely why more and more psychologists are embracing yoga as a complement to psychotherapy.

Research on Yoga as Therapy

In the November, 2009 issue of *Monitor on Psychology*, the article titled "Yoga as a Practice Tool" by Amy Novotney confirms the value of yoga practice as a natural solution to the mental health problem. Novotney cites studies by three different researchers.

There is clearly a need for improvement as the incidence of mental disorders has basically doubled among adults over a 10 year period. Not surprising, the use of psychotropic medication has risen at basically the same rate, according to a study by Sherry A. Glied, Ph.D. and Richard G. Frank, Ph.D.

Sat Bir Khalsa, Ph.D., is a neuroscientist and professor of medicine at Harvard Medical School at Brigham and Women's Hospital in Boston who studies yoga's effects on depression and insomnia. From his studies, the evidence indicates that yoga helps control unmanaged stress, the primary cause of numerous mental health problems. "It does this, he says, by reducing the stress response, which includes the activity of the sympathetic nervous system and the levels of the stress hormone cortisol. The practice enhances resilience and improves mind-body awareness, which can help people adjust their behaviors based on the feelings they're experiencing in their bodies, according to Khalsa."

This improved body awareness also can even help trauma survivor's deal with Post Traumatic Stress Disorder (PTSD). Ritu Sharma, Ph.D.; a coordinator of the Trauma Center at the Justice Resource Institute in Brookline, Mass., observed women with PTSD who took part in eight sessions of hatha yoga. These PTSD sufferers, as well as those studied by Richard Miller, (through research done with the Department of Defense), learn to focus on the present moment to become more aware of the sensations they are experiencing, thus reducing the severity of symptoms.

The benefits of yoga are not only derived from the actual physical practice, but the social environment of a yoga class has proven to be beneficial too. Kelly McGonigal, of Stanford University observes that "In a yoga class, everyone is moving and breathing at the same time and I think that's one of the undervalued mechanisms that yoga can really help with: giving people that sense of belonging, of being part of something bigger (http://www.apa.org/monitor/2009/11/yoga.aspx)."

Yoga for Anxiety and Depression

In order to create balance, it is essential to **START WHERE YOU ARE**. From a yogic perspective, energy can be sorted into three basic categories called *gunas*. The gunas are qualities of energy that exist in everything around us and within us.

Prana is the Sanskrit word for energy in yogic practices. Prana means inward (toward the center of your body) moving energy. Prana can be felt as you breathe in, expanding the thoracic cavity and lungs. It is often felt as an upward moving energy.

Apana (not prana) is the word for outward moving energy. It can be felt on the out breath and is often described as a downward moving energy.

Yoga means *union of body, mind, and spirit*. It is the state of consciousness and health where prana and apana are in harmony.

> **Tamas = low energy; not enough prana, too much apana**
>
> **Sattva = balanced energy**
>
> **Rajas = high energy; too much prana, not enough apana**

These qualities can be felt in everything around us: the weather, the food we eat, the moods and emotions we all experience, physical symptoms; all that is part of the rollercoaster ride of the human condition. Contentment is possible when we are balanced. This balance allows our *purusha* (spiritual energy), or inner light of awareness to shine out.

As with anything else in life, there are degrees to which energy can be observed. Simply noting your mental state throughout the day is a wise and loving way to care for yourself and begin to make some profound life changes.

A small letdown may be a one or a two on a zero to ten scale of disappointment that can lead to tamasic energy, whereas the grief from the loss of a loved one may be a ten. A small, pleasant surprise may be a two or three on the happiness (mild raja) scale, but winning the lotto may—at least initially—be a ten. When someone is depressed, it is felt as a deep heaviness or earthy experience, and when someone is anxious, it is felt as an extreme spacey or airy feeling. Finding the right breath work and physical practice to help oneself to become centered again is of utmost importance. A healthful diet and proper sleep are also essential. Contentment arises from balance.

Anxiety

Anxiety manifests when too much energy creates a rajasic state. The Sympathetic Nervous System (SNS) kicks in, and a myriad of physiological changes take place that affect the mind and the body. Anxiety is excessive energy, and often accompanies depression. The mind can be in a rajasic state, while the body is actually in a deeply depressed state. Anger is energy. In an episode of extreme anxiety or anger, it would likely not help to jump right into calming breath work (pranayama) or asana (posture). Note how rapidly you are breathing. When too much oxygen is getting to the brain and not enough carbon dioxide is being released, it is not surprising how dramatic the effect is on the body and mind. Walking can help. Regulating the breath while walking, or doing a vigorous practice (such as sun salutations) can allow one to burn off the excess energy to slowly progress to the floor. This will bring the anxiety slowly under control—into a feeling of steadiness; ultimately to a place of calm and peace. Anger and anxiety are both energy. Once under control, each can be put to good use; they can be transformative for the individual and for society.

Yoga Asanas for Anxiety

When experiencing anxiety, once the excess anger/anxiety is "burned off" from doing something physical, forward bends and inversions can be helpful, such as:

~ Spread out foot posture	~ Seated forward bend	~ Child's Pose
~ Seated head to knee	~ Shoulderstand	~ Headstand

Pranayamas for Anxiety

~ Ujjayi pranayama (victorious breath)

~ Nadi Shodana pranayama (alternate nostril breathing)

~ Any pranayama that creates a ratio to slowly lengthen the exhalation is recommended. Once stability is achieved, one can then begin to even the breath

Yoga Sequence to Manage Anxiety Disorders

The following sequence is from BKS Iyengar's *Light on Yoga* and was found at www.holisticonline.com B.K.S. Iyengar recommends the following yoga *sequence to manage anxiety.

1. Mountain pose or equal standing

2. Upward stretch

3. Forward bend

4. Triangle pose

5. Spread out foot posture: Turn from straddle to the front of the mat to step back to plank to lower to your belly. Take a gentle cobra to

6. Downward facing dog; come to seated for

7. Seated forward bend

8. Seated straddle

9. Shoulderstand and/or legs up the wall pose

10. Corpse pose

*Advanced asanas were removed from the original sequence.

Depression

In cases of moderate, chronic depression, referred to as dysthymic disorder, yoga practices can create significantly positive changes in energy level. Learning to note the breath allows the student to recognize how shallow the in-breath has become and how long the out-breath typically is when in a state of low energy or depression. The result: not enough oxygen to the brain and too much carbon dioxide being released.

In cases of more severe depression, it is not reasonable for one to feel up to doing a moderately-paced or vigorous yoga practice that could be beneficial in getting energy moving. Therefore, starting on the floor with gentle postures would be the best place to begin. Moving slowly while focusing on creating a breath ratio in which the inhalation is longer than the exhalation is a wonderful way to start moving the energy.

When someone is experiencing major depressive disorder, it is all that he or she can do to even consider getting out of bed to face the world. In these cases, it is imperative that one get medical help. The desire to help oneself has to precede the methods that yoga practice can offer to help one pull out of the cave of depression. For the person who is depressed, it is often the guilt associated with the discrepancy between how they actually feel and how they (or others) think they should feel that exacerbates the problem.

Yoga Asanas Recommended for Depression

Poses that open the heart and arch the back create more flow of energy through the body. The following back bends are recommended for depression as long as there are no contraindications:

~ Cobra	~ Bow	~ Modified bridge	~ Full bridge	~ Fish

Pranayamas for Depression

Any pranayama that allows the inhalation to be lengthened could be of great value. There are now many studies done on particular Kriyas and pranayama in the Kundalini tradition due to studies being done at Harvard by Dr. Sat Bir Singh Khalsa. Once a balance is achieved from lengthening the in-breath, an even breath ratio can sustain the balance.

A Yoga Sequence to Manage Depression

1. Rising from child's pose to upward facing stretch from knees or from a chair. This is sometimes called "flying cow" but may best be described as "blossoming child"

2. 3–5X sun salutations from the knees or from a chair

3. Move to prone position for bow pose for 5-10 breaths

4. Child's pose for 3–5 breaths

5. Cat/cow 3–5 X and lower to supine position

6. Bridging 1–5 X for 3–5 breaths each time

7. Shoulderstand or legs up the wall pose for 5–15 breaths

8. Fish pose for 3–5 breaths OR done as a restorative pose for 3–5 minutes with a bolster

9. Corpse pose (savasana) for 5–10 minutes

In addition to the suggested progressive muscle relaxation below, these meditation techniques and pranayama varieties are helpful: metta (loving kindness) meditation, walking meditation, breath of joy, and…hugs.

Yoga Relaxation Exercise for Depression

Try the following progressive muscle relaxation (tension and release exercise) as you lie in the Corpse Pose:

- As you inhale through your nose, tighten the muscles in legs from the quads down to the toes. Hold the tension, then relax and exhale.

- Inhale, tensing all of the previous body parts as well as your abdomen, low back, pelvic floor, and buttocks. Hold them taut, then relax and exhale.

- Tense the muscles in your neck, shoulders, arms, hands, fingers, chest as well as muscles in your trunk and legs. Hold the tension, then relax and exhale.

- Finally, starting with your scalp, face, and head, tense all of the muscles you can, all the way down to the toes. Hold the tension, then relax and exhale. Feel how all of the tension has melted away from your body.

 ## Yoga Nidra for Anxiety, Depression, and Post Traumatic Stress Disorder (PTSD)

Yoga Nidra has been found to have compelling results for people experiencing anxiety and depression from Post Traumatic Stress Disorder, or PTSD. The difficulty in beginning to use such a technique is that one must be able to get relaxed enough to be able to sit or recline for the techniques to be practiced. Yoga Nidra is a specific form of meditation. Ancient texts have equated Yoga Nidra to *samadhi*, or the eighth limb of Ashtanga Yoga, which represents the penultimate goal of yoga, enlightenment. Reduced to the simplest description, it is a form of meditation that resembles progressive relaxation where the practitioner gradually relaxes specific parts of his or her body. As the body begins to relax, emotions and thoughts typically arise. Richard Miller, a renowned yoga instructor and clinical psychologist, believes that the ability to welcome and observe these emotions and thoughts helps the meditator become less identified with his or her individual self which can lead to deep relaxation. This form of meditation has been proven to help a wide variety of individuals including those that are dealing with different forms of mental illness.

"Researchers are examining the practice's potential to help soldiers suffering from post-traumatic stress disorder; addicts struggling to get clean; people with depression, cancer, and MS; health care workers; and married couples coping with stress and insomnia." A number of studies have indicated that Yoga Nidra maybe helpful for active and retired members of the armed services who are dealing with Post Traumatic Stress Disorder (PTSD). Miller somewhat "westernized" the practice and refers to it as Integrative Restoration or iRest. Soldiers who have participated in the iRest programs have reported the reduction of many of the symptoms of PTSD including hyperalertness, anxiety, and sleep disturbances.

A study evaluating the potential benefits of Dr. Miller's iRest yoga nidra program for the reduction of stress among college students (iRest Yoga-Nidra on the College Campus Changes in Stress, Depression, Worry, and Mindfulness. Eastman-Mueller) demonstrated that students were able to reduce perceived stress and worries as well as decrease the effects of depression. In addition, students improved their mindfulness skills including nonreactivity to inner experience, observing/noticing/attending to perceptions/feelings/thoughts, acting with awareness, describing/labeling with words, and nonjudging of the experience.

 ## Bipolar Disorder

The power of yoga asana and pranayama to bring the body and mind to a more balanced place is incredibly valuable to anyone who suffers from the fluctuations of mood and energy created by bipolar disorder. Additionally, the philosophy of Yoga is a remarkable method for navigating mental illness. When fluctuations of energy and mood are noted, there are things that can be done to rectify the situation. Positive thinking, and various postures and rates of breath allow one to meet the energy where it is and work from there. Over time and practice, this can be empowering and comforting to anyone suffering from any type of mental illness.

 ## Research to Support Yoga and Chanting

The May 2012 issue of *Medical Hypotheses* journal featured the results of a study done by a team of researchers at Boston University School of Medicine. The study, "The Effects of Yoga on the Autonomic Nervous System, Gamma-aminobutric-acid, and Allostasis in Epilepsy, Depression, and Post-Traumatic Stress Disorder" focused on the importance of the tone of the vagus nerve. The study shines a light on how and why yoga asana, pranayama, and chanting (or singing) can benefit a yoga practitioner.

Dr. Chris Streeter and his team found that yoga breathing, specifically ujjayi breathing, and chanting "Om" out loud helped to increase vagal nerve tone. The vagas nerve begins at the base of the skull and wanders throughout the body, affecting the nervous system, the digestive system and the respiratory system, thus helping to regulate all of our bodily systems. This research truly shines a light on how and why yoga asana, pranayama, and chanting (or singing) can benefit a yoga practitioner. (From Yoga International.com Winter 2013-14)

According to the National Institute of Mental Health (NIMH) brain stimulation therapies hold promise for people who do not show improvement from conventional treatments such as anti-depressants, light therapy, and psychotherapy. One of the five Brain Stimulation Therapies (BST) being researched by the NIMH is Vagus Nerve Stimulation, or VNS, which was approved by the Food and Drug Administration in 2005 to treat people with major depression. This particular treatment is only used when a patient has not responded to conventional treatments and has had major depression for two years or more.

While these brain stimulation treatment methods are not without side effects, the result of the studies done thus far warrant more exploration. Studies are ongoing and will eventually show the efficacy of these treatments for mood disorders.

Numerous studies done on the power of vibration from chanting have been done which show that the vagus nerve, when stimulated, can bring about significant changes in brain chemistry that have been shown to help people with major depressive disorders. While more studies are needed to determine the value of chanting for those with various physical and psychological disorders, but two things are clear:

1. The side effects appear to be mainly positive, and

2. Chanting is free

Om or "Aum" is a sacred syllable/sound/intonation/mantra/prayer/primordial vibration that represents omnipotence and omnipresence. It embodies both the unmanifest and manifest aspects of what your personal concept of God may be: Divine Consciousness; Love; Nature; the Absolute; Supreme Consciousness; etc. The past, the present, and the future, all potentialities and possibilities, are encapsulated within this one sound. It is believed to be the basic sound of the world; containing all other sounds within the universe, including the sounds of all the languages spoken on earth.

Om is woven all through life and is in our life force, or breath. Chanting AUM with the proper intonation allows the sound to resonate throughout the body. This creates and moves incredible vibration (energy) which may indeed have healing implications.

Although Om symbolizes the most profound concepts of Hindu belief, it is used daily by most yoga practitioners, as a reminder of the commitment one is making toward the cultivation of peace in his or her life.

While the concepts within this symbol and its many expressions are indeed profound and beautiful, there are religions that look upon the symbol and it's concepts as uncomfortable, if not threatening. This may be due to the fact that the ideas precede, and therefore do not fit the framework of these particular religions.

In recent years, people have created numerous works of art that portray the symbol of "Om" (ॐ). While this may be done simply as a fashion statement for some, for others it may be a reminder of the deep peace they wish to cultivate. The benevolence and tolerance of Hinduism would likely not look down on such displays since the intention behind the action, whether egotistic or not, is infinitesimal in comparison to the concept.

Yoga Is for Everybody and Every Body

Through the years most students have found yoga to be a wonderful form of exercise and preventative "medicine", while others discovered it to be a lifestyle or recognized it as a spiritual path.

This is one of the many beautiful things about the practice of yoga. It can be any one (or all) of these things. The choice is yours. No matter what your original intention was for taking a yoga class, most of you will likely come away with at least some new "tools" in your belt, and quite possibly a profound sense of presence and peace.

Over the years I have heard so many wonderful comments from students about how the practice affected their health, relationships, sense of spirituality, sense of community, athletic ability and more.

Numerous athletes representing all of the sports here at WCU have reported a decrease in injuries, an increase in strength and flexibility and an improvement in the ability to focus and use breath to keep stress levels under control before, during, and after competition.

In addition, surfers, rock climbers, runners, equestrians, tennis players, golfers, dancers, snowboarders, skaters, etc.; whether performing competitively or not, have expressed that the practice of yoga had improved their athletic endeavors dramatically.

Musicians, singers, and theatre majors have commented on the value of the breathing exercises of yoga in particular, and generally speaking, students find the practice of yoga to be an invaluable new tool that will eventually complement the field in which they came to school to study.

Goodluz/Shutterstock.com   Monkey Business Images/   bikeriderlondon/Shutterstock.com
                                  Shutterstock.com

Yoga is for everybody and for every BODY.

One semester in particular highlights the significance of yoga practice for a wide variety of students. In 2005, in a class of thirty five students, there was an obese student, many overweight students, a student with a broken ankle, a few students with serious health issues, and…the star running back from the football team. There were type A personalities, type B personalities, all body types, and all the issues that go with these—ranging from an intensely competitive elite athlete, to individuals struggling with self-esteem and severe weight issues, and yet, the end of semester evaluations proved that yoga benefitted all thirty-five of them!

Grace Galore

Everybody walks around with grace in his or her life.

There is no person in whose life it is not present.

Indeed, our very existence is an expression of grace.

The problem is that we don't recognize what it is,

and even if we have connected to it,

we usually don't have the skill to sustain the connection.

There is only surrendering ourselves into stillness—

And that is where we meet up with grace.

—Swami Chetanananda

WILL I BE THE HERO OF MY OWN LIFE?

 **Going Deeper**

If you are currently experiencing symptoms of depression and/or anxiety, consider a visit to your school counselor, counseling center, or wellness center for further assistance. Most, if not all, high schools and universities have wonderful resources for their students. Take a deep breath and call.

A link of interest:

http://www.health.harvard.edu/newsletters/Harvard_Mental_Health_Letter/2009/April/Yoga-for-anxiety-and-depression

Ashtanga Yoga: The Eight-Limbed Path to Union of Body, Mind, and Spirit

Why not go out on a limb? Isn't that where the fruit is?

—Frank Scully

 ## Patanjali's Eight-Limbed Path

The eight-limbed path put forth by Patanjali in the *Yoga Sutras* often is depicted as a ladder, with each of the eight steps representing the different aspects of Yoga. The top rung of the ladder symbolizes enlightenment.

The only problem with this characterization is that you rarely, if ever, proceed in a sequential manner through the limbs of Yoga. Nor were the limbs intended to be explored one step at a time. The limbs of Yoga are more like a beautiful tapestry, connected by the very fabric and threads from which it is woven.

A more accurate depiction of the limbs of yoga would be like actual limbs on a tree. When the roots and trunk of the tree (the yamas and niyamas) are firmly established and strong, the other limbs can grow upward toward the light (enlightenment).

Patanjali's eight-limbed path, or Ashtanga Yoga, recorded in the *Yoga Sutras* is as follows:

1. **Yama:** The five yamas are social restraints or ethical values—ahimsa (nonviolence), satya (truthfulness), asteya (nonstealing), brahmacharya (moderation), and aparigraha (greedlessness, nonhoarding, nongrasping).

2. **Niyama:** The five niyamas are personal observances—saucha (cleanliness), santosha (contentment), tapas (the burning of impurities through intensity), svadhaya (self-study), and ishvara pranidhana (surrender to a higher power).

3. **Asana:** The physical postures of Yoga.

4. **Pranayama:** Breath control and regulation.

5. **Pratyahara:** Withdrawing the senses in order to prepare for deep concentration.

6. **Dharana:** Unwavering concentration.

7. **Dhyana:** Meditation; conscious awareness.

8. **Samadhi:** Higher consciousness; a state of bliss.

 # Limb 1: The Yamas

Imagine all the people living life in peace...you may say I'm a dreamer, but I'm not the only one, I hope someday you will join us, and the world will live as one.

—John Lennon

The yamas are the moral codes of attitude and conduct that a true yogin would live by. They are often referred to as "restraints".

They are as follows:

Ahimsa: Nonviolence

Satya: Truthfulness

Asteya: Nonstealing

Brahmacharya: Moderation in all things

Aparigraha: nonhoarding

Ahimsa

Watch your thoughts, for they become words.
Watch your words, for they become actions.
Watch your actions, for they become habits.
Watch your habits, for they become character.
Watch your character, for it becomes your destiny.

From The Upanishads (an ancient Yogic text)

One of the resources used to create this chapter is *YogaLife: 10 Steps to Freedom*, a wonderful little book written by Johanna Maheshvari Mosca, Ph.D.

Living by the principle of ahimsa, you should choose thoughts, words, and actions with utmost care so as not to harm yourself or others. In your asana practice, follow ahimsa by finding your "edge" in the posture and staying there. We violate this principle in asana practice when we push ourselves into a posture to the point of experiencing pain.

Many yoga practitioners choose to become vegetarians in order to practice ahimsa fully. This will be explored further in Chapter 10.

Thoughts to Ponder

Please answer the following questions:

1. Are you kind to yourself?

2. In what ways are you kind to yourself? In what ways are you unkind to yourself?

3. How could you treat yourself with more kindness and compassion?

4. Are you kind to others? In what ways are you kind to others?

5. In what ways are you unkind to others?

6. How could you treat others with more kindness and compassion?

Common Violations of Ahimsa

Negative Thinking   How many thoughts that you think on a daily basis do you suppose are kind? Necessary? True? Helpful? Important? How much is just garbage?

Thousands of years ago, Patanjali said that our energy goes where our mind goes. Where is your energy going? How much of *your* vital energy are you wasting on stink'n think'n?

Anytime we engage in negative self-talk, we reinforce neural pathways in the brain, making it more and more difficult to break the patterns of thought and the brain chemistry they create. As you are likely aware, our conditioned thoughts become our conditioned behaviors. The Sanskrit word for these patterns is *samskara*. Interestingly, this word sounds similar to "some scars." The next time you catch yourself thinking unkind thoughts about yourself, *stop*. Take a deep breath and ask yourself: "Is it kind? Is it even true in the first place?"

If a pattern is particularly strong, it has become more or less an unconscious blueprint. As soon as you wake up to the fact that you can indeed change your thoughts, you have taken the giant leap forward to living more consciously.

Negative Speech   When we speak in a way that is negative or harmful to ourselves or to others, we are consciously or unconsciously violating ahimsa. Gossip is a common infringement, as is shouting unkind things in traffic or during an athletic competition. Take deep breaths instead. Choose kindness. You will rarely, if ever, regret choosing kindness. The truth is, you have no idea what the other person may be going through in his or her life. Who are you to judge and criticize? Or as Wayne Dyer says, "When you judge another you do not define them, you define yourself."

Negative Actions   When we physically harm ourselves or others, we go against ahimsa. When food or drink is consumed in excess, when we don't give our bodies and minds the proper rest and nutrition required to run smoothly, we are in violation of this concept. If ever in a situation where a physical confrontation seems inevitable, can you choose to walk away?

The next time your knee-jerk reaction to seeing a harmless bug, for example, is to crush it, choose instead to let it climb onto a finger (or a brave friend's finger) and take it outside. Instead of spraying chemical pesticides inside or outside your living space, try instead to find a way to avoid that course of action in the first place, such as keeping your living space cleaner to avoid rodents or bugs.

There are, of course, exceptions to the above suggestions. If, for instance, you play a defensive position on an athletic team, or are defending another person or group of people from harm; or you are allergic to bees and there is one flying around your living space; obviously, it would be reasonable to assume that you would have to work around some of these proposals.

Practicing ahimsa is a challenge in this day and age. If you drive a fuel-efficient car, live sustainably, and are kind to yourself and others, but you think or speak negatively about those who do not follow a similar path, you are still infringing on this yama.

Keep in mind that Adolf Hitler read the *Vedas* and was a vegetarian. Even though he subscribed to some lovely precepts, he was responsible for the commitment of atrocious and unconscionable crimes against humankind.

Satya

> Speak the truth which is pleasant. Do not speak unpleasant truths. Do not lie, even if the lies are pleasing to the ear.
>
> —From the Mahabharata

Living in accordance with satya, a student of Yoga would choose thoughts, words, and actions with care and consideration of self and others. A person who practices satya is able to "walk his or

her talk." When practicing yoga asana, the individual would refrain from trying going deeper in a posture that was not yet comfortable.

Thoughts to Ponder

Please answer the following questions:

1. Do you speak the truth to yourself?

2. Do you speak the truth to others?

3. Are you living in a way that is truthful to your beliefs?

4. What will you need to do in order to be more truthful to yourself and others?

Common Violations of Satya

- Thinking or saying anything aloud that is not true.
- Staying in a relationship that is damaging to yourself or the other person.
- Being unfaithful in a committed relationship.
- Working in a job that you don't believe in.
- Not practicing what you preach.

Asteya

Every gun that is made, every warship launched, every rocket fired, signifies in the final sense a theft from those who hunger and are not fed, and those who are cold and not clothed.

—Dwight David Eisenhower, 34th American President

To live in harmony with asteya, you strive to take only what is needed and no more, and continue to make choices that encourage simplicity. We are now beginning to realize the truth in Gandhi's words: "The world has enough for everyone's need, but not enough for everyone's greed." We have begun to contemplate that the world's resources are finite and what may happen if we continue to consume at the current pace. Overconsumption coupled with continued overpopulation will be stifling at best, if not brought under control.

In the United States alone, estimates are that there are now over thirty million people, over one-third of whom are children who go to bed hungry each night. In a land with so much, how can this be?

If you are like most people, you probably find it appalling that a coffee shop can charge four dollars for a latte, yet many of the farmers who harvested those beans live in poverty and cannot send their children to school. If U.S. schoolchildren had any idea that slave laborers (most of whom are children) harvested the cocoa beans in the chocolate bars and chocolate eggs that they are given during various holidays, would they want to eat them?

On a much lighter note—in terms of daily activities and behaviors—if we work on being considerate of others by refraining from stealing their time and energy, and if we are mindful to return any borrowed item(s) as quickly as possible, we are in accord with asteya. Regarding your yoga asana practice, avoid trying to go deeper in a yoga pose when the previous one was all you needed to feel good.

Thoughts to Ponder

Please answer the following questions:

1. Do you put more food on your plate than what you really need?

2. Do you waste food, water, electricity, or any other resource?

3. Are you considerate of other people's time? Is there anyone who is not considerate of your time?

4. Do you ruin someone's good energy by sharing negative stories and problems?

5. Is there someone in your life who steals (time, energy, resources) from you?

6. Do you take items from your job or from restaurants? Remember: Time spent socializing when you are being paid to do a job is stealing and…those sugar packets from your favorite restaurant are not yours!

Common Violations of Asteya

- A teacher who consistently keeps you well over the allotted class time
- A doctor who consistently leaves people waiting for long periods for appointments
- Telling someone that you will "be right there" and then not following through
- Gossiping or generally speaking negatively
- Speaking on the phone, texting, computer or TV viewing while spending planned social time with someone or a group of people
- Taking more (of anything) than what is needed
- Taking something that does not belong to you

Brahmacharya

This yama has ultimately to do with sexual restraint. The intention behind brahmacharya is not to ruin our sex life. Instead, brahmacharya allow us to view our sexuality as the primal force that it is. Through the practice of brahmacharya, we learn how to harness our sexuality and use it in ways that do no harm to ourselves and others. There is a great deal of self-respect and satisfaction that will come from resisting, rather than yielding to, a *wrong* desire. Certainly, this is not to say that all sexual desires are wrong.

Another way of looking at this yama relates to moderation. When we practice moderation of even the pleasurable things in life, we avoid becoming overly attached, obsessed, or addicted to the satisfaction that these things bring. When we learn to observe sensory stimulation and apply moderation, we learn to remain focused on our purpose in life.

Thoughts to Ponder

Please answer the following questions:

1. Do you practice moderation in speech? Do you often say more than you need to say, or say things you later regret saying?

2. Are your actions a reflection of moderation?

3. Do you have good time management skills?

4. In a monogamous relationship, do you flirt with others?

The circle below represents a twenty-four-hour day. Where do you spend most of your energy? Slice up this "energy pie" with all current daily activities. This means anything (watching television, texting, eating, driving, etc.) that you spend any time at all doing. Use the side of the circle to record activities, and then place them in a slice representative of the time spent on that activity.

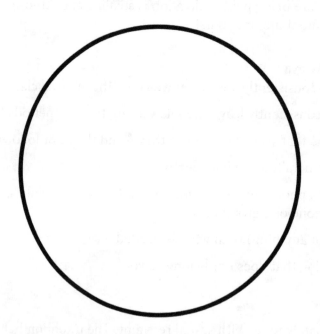

Do you like the way this looks?

Now, slice up the "perfect day." What would your perfect day realistically look like in terms of energy spent?

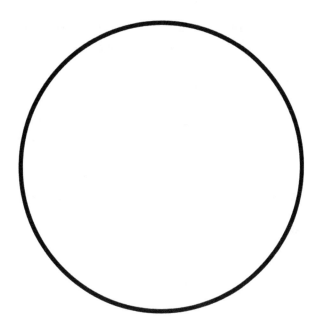

Aparigraha

In the end, these things matter the most:
How deeply did you love?
How fully did you live?
How completely did you learn to let go?

—Siddhartha Gautama, The Buddha

None of us gets out of this (life) alive. Every day we experience hundreds of little letting-go's. The great opportunity in practicing aparigraha is that we begin to learn to recognize what is not working in our lives. We learn to let go of the little stuff, consequently making it easier to let go of the bigger stuff. Death, of course, is the ultimate letting go. In the philosophy of Yoga, the fear of death is considered to be one of the things that can really hold us back in learning to live our lives fully (Abhinivesha). Attachment to anything that is impermanent is considered a sign of ignorance (Avidya), which of course, does not mean stupidity, but rather a state of unawareness.

In *The Mantram Handbook* (1998), written by the late Ecknath Easwaran—author, spiritual teacher, Fulbright Scholar and Professor at the University of California, Berkeley—offers a poignant story related to this final letting go. Easwaren tells of his grandmother taking him along with her as she would deliver food to, and visit with, people in their community who were sick. Some were dying. Ecknath, a young boy at the time, asked her why death should involve so much suffering. She instructed him to go and sit in a large wooden chair in their home and to hold on as tightly as possible to the chair. His grandmother then proceeded to pull him out of the chair with great force. When he told her that this had hurt him, she replied, "Let's try it again." This time, however, he was instructed not to hold on. With no struggle or pain, she lifted him effortlessly into her arms.

Wouldn't life be so much easier if we could learn to stop holding on so tightly?

When a student begins to practice aparigraha, he or she learns to distinguish between wants and needs. Between what works and what doesn't. What is truly needed (food, shelter, clothing, love) and what the senses often are craving or wanting. As awareness of the tendencies of greed, grasping, and hoarding are observed, the individual then has the presence of mind to practice contentment with what *is*, rather than always giving in to desires based on *wants*.

We often want *someone* to be different, and we will end up wasting a good deal of energy trying to get that person to think or behave as *we* would. If we always want this new item, that new relationship, this new hair color, that new car, that new pair of shoes, etc., we are basically saying that things are not all right as they are. We are not okay as we are. The world is not providing for us. We cannot trust that we are being taken care of.

People may have control issues and desire to "fix" things for others. This is a violation (whether conscious or unconscious) of aparigraha. Additionally, people who hoard possessions and have a hard time letting go of them are violating this principle.

People hold on to all kinds of things that they no longer need. Clothes that were never worn or no longer fit. All kinds of material things. Relationships that no longer work. Even thoughts that no longer (or never) worked.

An exception to the concept of letting go would, of course, be in terms of injustices.

Thoughts to Ponder

Please answer the questions below:

1. Who are you? Use as many adjectives as you like.

2. Who are you? Strip away all of the qualifiers and adjectives above.

3. Why do you believe you are here? On Earth.

4. Which material items that you currently possess do you feel you would have a hard time letting go of? Why?

5. To whom would you wish to give these items when you no longer need them? Why did you select this person?

6. Which relationships or people in your life will you have difficulty in letting go of? Why?

7. If you knew you had twenty-four hours to live, with whom would you want to be? Where would you spend those hours?

Limb 2: The Niyamas

The niyamas are observances, or ways of operating in the world. A bit more personal than the yamas, the niyamas help us to create a healthy environment and shape our attitudes about ourselves and the world we live in.

Saucha

Saucha means purity, or cleanliness in thought, word and deed. It relates to both inner and outer cleanliness. Sound easy?

Consider, and answer the following questions, if you wish:

1. Is your living space clean and well organized?

2. Do you use good personal hygiene?

3. Do you think, speak, and act in a positive manner?

4. Do you eat clean, fresh food that is good for your body and mind?

5. Do you find yourself often feeling angry, envious, jealous, or prideful?

6. Do you engage in activities that are good for your mental and physical health?

In *Yoga Unveiled* (2004), a yoga documentary, author and teacher, Dr. Georg Feuerstein refers to saucha when he speaks about the obsession that many Americans have with purification of the body. His words imply the futility of purifying the body with no regard to thoughts and speech when he states, "We are body/minds that talk. How can one work without the other?"

In Cat De Rham and Michelle Gill's beautiful book, *The Spirit of Yoga* (2001), saucha is epitomized in the following statement: "The entire search for our true essence is a process of purification and letting go. As the impurities dissolve, the light of self-knowledge and awareness emerges. The energy of the universes circulates freely."

Samtosa

This niyama, also spelled santosha, is about cultivating a feeling of gratitude and contentment. Even during times in our lives where we are faced with a difficult truth, such as losing a loved one or being denied an opportunity we looked forward to exploring, can we *still* find it in ourselves to accept and move on in our lives?

Consider, and answer if you wish, these questions:

1. What are you grateful for on this day?

2. Was there ever a time in your life when things did not go as planned but actually ended up serving you well (in your evolution as a human being)?

Affirmations or a personal mantra can be a valuable resources in practicing contentment. The simple act of repeating a positive statement, whether aloud or silently, is a gesture of compassion and self-love that can serve us well in life.

An interesting thing to note: When we begin to give more of what it is we feel is missing in our lives (nonmaterial), we often find we stop missing it altogether. Why? Because what we give comes back. As Osho once said in a lecture to his students, later to be recorded in the book, *Everyday Osho* (2002), "The world is an echoing place. If we throw anger, anger comes back; if we give love, love comes back."

Most of the simple affirmations below were obtained from author Louise Hay:

I am loving, lovable, and loved
I am at peace
Smile
Breathe
I live with intention
I am patient
I am kind
My life unfolds perfectly before me
I am safe
I breathe love into my vision
I see with compassion
I am grateful for this wonderful day

Tapas

Dig into yourself for a deep answer. And if this answer rings out in assent, if you meet this solemn question with a strong, simple, 'I must,' then build your life in accordance with this necessity; your whole life, even down to its humblest and most indifferent hour, must be a sign and witness to this impulse.

—Rainier Maria Rilke

Tapas is a Sanskrit word that is often defined in terms of heat; burning the impurities through asana and pranayama to keep our body and mind fit. It also implies an effort to remain unaffected by opposites, thus learning how to confront inner urges gracefully. The practice of tapas involves intense discipline to develop healthy habits, prevent disease, and pursue our life's purpose.

Svadhaya

This niyama means self-study—intentionally learning more about yourself in order to grow and evolve spiritually. Your Hatha yoga practice will be one of your greatest teachers. It sounds difficult, but all that self-inquiry truly requires is our attention. We must pay attention.

We learn through self-inquiry how to let go of destructive tendencies and how to nurture the constructive ones. As we become more centered—present for ourselves and our lives—we can live with heart and from the heart to reach our full potential in life.

The process of self-study also requires us to continue to learn and better ourselves through scholarly study.

Ishvarapranidhana

This niyama stands for the concept that there is a force that is larger than us, whether you call that force God, universal consciousness, Divine wisdom, Nature, or something else. This limb allows us to explore the idea that we are microcosms of the macrocosm; we are a smaller part of the larger whole. From this perspective, everything is connected, and we can surrender to that to experience the grace of being alive. As Shiva Rea (2002) so eloquently states in "The Practice of

Surrender," an online *Yoga Journal* article, "Ishvara pranidhana provides a pathway through the obstacles of our ego toward our divine nature-grace, peace, unconditional love, clarity and freedom."

Limb 3: Asana

Asana means seat or posture. In the *Yoga Sutras*, Patanjali mentioned very little pertaining specifically to the physical postures of yoga, very likely because he was describing asana as a position in which one would meditate. One of the important things that *is* mentioned, however, is in reference to *how* asana should be performed. Patanjali used the words *sukha* and *sthira* to describe the qualities we should be able to observe in a posture.

According to Robert Svoboda and Scott Blossom in the article, "Balancing Ourselves in Good Space," sthira can mean "firm, compact, strong, steadfast, resolute, courageous; arising from the root *stha*, which means "to take a firm stand." Sukha means "happy, good, joyful, delightful, easy, agreeable, gentle, mild, and virtuous." The literal meaning is "good space," from the root words *su* (good) and *kha* (space). When we create these qualities in our asana practice, we develop the state of mind that facilitates this balance in all aspects of our lives.

While asana may have originally been intended as a posture that one would meditate in, through the years Patanjali's instructions have been adopted by most, if not all, traditions of Hatha yoga to create the qualities of steadiness and ease throughout even the most intense asana practice.

Asana will be explored further in Chapter 6 and 7.

Limb 4: Pranayama

This aspect of yoga has to do with learning to control (ayama) our life force, or breath (prana). One could spend an entire lifetime learning about this limb of yoga. You will likely discover that learning even a few basic varieties of pranayama will be invaluable. Nothing affects our state of mind quite as dramatically as the quality of our breath. Pranayama will be explored further in Chapters 6, 7, and 8. We will only be practicing basic breathing exercises, as it requires a highly trained teacher to help one to pursue this limb more deeply.

Limb 5: Pratyahara

Pratyahara, the fifth limb of the eight-limbed path, is the bridge that leads to meditation. Limb five is the cultivation of sense control that creates an awakening of individual sense awareness. When we learn to control the senses, the senses can no longer control us.

David Swenson has referred to a horse-drawn chariot as the perfect analogy: a chariot pulled by five horses (senses), which are reined in by the driver (mind) of the chariot (body). According to Beryl Bender Birch, in *Beyond Power Yoga* (2000), pratyahara is a state of consciousness that cannot be created; it just happens when we are steady and focused.

Pratyahara is sometimes described as being "in the zone"; a moment (or moments) in time where there seems to be no such thing as time. In asana practice, if we allow intelligence, rather than ego, to guide us, we are able experience this sense of timelessness. We develop this ability to control the senses through dedication and commitment to a regular practice.

Limbs 6, 7, and 8: Dharana, Dhyana, and Samadhi

In the *Yoga Sutras*, Patanjali refers to the last three limbs of yoga as aspects of practice which all have to do with control. All should be considered together as there are no actual dividing lines between them. One leads to another.

Limb six, dharana, is deep concentration; unwavering attention on a fixed object. The previous limb, pratyahara, develops the ability to experience dharana, as it would be difficult to hold complete concentration if the senses were still tugging us around.

One of the two main foes of dharana is boredom, but witnessing the boredom will lead you to recognize that you really are not bored at all. Focusing deeply is amazingly interesting.

The other antagonist is fear. Certainly, not all fear is bad. We need to be safe. But the reality for most of us is that many of our fears are unfounded. Self-generated fear too often becomes an obstacle that ends up holding us back from experiencing the heart of the matter. Neale Donald Walsch is known for creating the following acronym for fear (**www.essentialawareness.org/neale-donald-walsch-discusses-the-emotion-of-fear.php**—United Kingdom):

FALSE	EVIDENCE	APPEARING	REAL

From their book The Spirit of Yoga, Cat De Rham and Michele Gill make the following observations:

We never really encounter the world. What we experience is our own nervous system reacting to the world.

Physics teaches us that everything is energy and that at its deepest level are things are interconnected.

We see things as separate because of the limitation of our senses. This sense of separateness is an illusion.

The Self is beyond the senses. It stands apart—free and knowing. To experience the Self-this infinite reality beneath the world of the senses-our consciousness needs to shine inwards away from external stimuli.

This is the slow journey away from the duality of the senses and the mind, to unity and stillness.

To a soul that has poise.

Through dharana, your perception of the object of attention will change through your steadfast awareness. When an object of awareness is viewed through the lens of dharana, its pure essence will be revealed. When we have attained unwavering attention, we can then experience dhyana, the seventh limb of yoga.

Dhyana can be translated as meaning contemplation or meditation; it is conscious awareness. When the object of meditation and the meditator are one, we move into a state of inner bliss referred to as samadhi.

Samadhi, the eighth limb of yoga is the highest state of consciousness known as "oneness," or enlightenment. It is described as a spiritual experience in which there is a merging of the soul with the collective consciousness of the universe.

The ancient yogis believed that our true nature is one of peace, pure love, and joy. It is only when we strip away the layers upon layers of conditioned existence that we can reach this beautiful space…*our* essence. From this perspective, love is not a fleeting emotion, but rather a state of consciousness that allows us to see and live with compassion.

Truth is not far away. It is nearer than near. There is no need to attain it since not one of our steps leads away from it.

—Dogen

Test Your Knowledge

Name _____ **Date** _____

1. Briefly summarize each of the five yamas.

    1.

    2.

    3.

    4.

    5.

2. Record five ways you could incorporate the yamas into your life. Please be specific and use <u>personal examples</u>.

3. Briefly summarize the niyamas.

    1.

    2.

    3.

    4.

    5.

4. Record five ways you could incorporate the niyamas into your life. Please be specific and use personal examples.

5. According to Patanjali, what are the qualities that asana(s) should possess?

6. What does the word *pranayama* mean?

7. What is pratyahara?

8. How does a yoga student develop pratyahara?

9. Briefly describe the last three limbs of yoga.

Yama "OMwork"

For 1 day this week:

- **Practice the following quote** by Sai Baba: "Before you speak, ask yourself, is it kind, is it necessary, is it true? Will it improve on the silence?"

- **Create and practice an affirmation** based on Gandhi's quote: "Be the change you want to see in the world." Create your own affirmation:

- Today I will be _____. Fill in the blank with what it is you wish to see in the world.

How did it impact your day? Please journal your experience. If the result was positive, do it again tomorrow. And the next day. And the next day…

- **Pack up a bag of clothing or other items you no longer use and take it to the Salvation Army or another charitable drop center.**

Niyama "OMwork"

- **Clean your room**. Just do it. You know you will feel better.

- **Create a gratitude journal**. Keep it beside your bed. For one week, immediately upon rising, record three things you are grateful for. In the evening, before you go to sleep, record three more. Examine what you have recorded at the end of the week. At the end of the week, record your experience.

- **Every day, for one week: create ten minutes (same time each day, preferably) to sit and breathe.** Journal your experience daily, and review your entries at the end of the week.

- **Do an Internet search for affirmations. Record ten to twenty that resonate with you.**

- **Find a soothing mantra, and practice it throughout the day for one week**. If it is helpful, adopt that mantra for daily use.

Asana "OMwork"

- **Explore** www.Yogajournal.com or www.yogainternational.com by searching the anatomical focus link for postures that can improve the areas of your body that you personally feel to be weak or inflexible; or search any asana that pertains to emotional issues you feel need resolution. Put the information into a document, or print to create a binder for your personal use throughout the semester and beyond.

- **Locate yoga studios close by and sample different classes and styles of yoga.**

Pranayama "OMwork"

- **Research a variety of pranayamas** for a condition or circumstance that has personal significance, such as improving asthma, reducing anxiety, creating relaxation, etc.

Pratayahara "OMwork"

- ~ Close your eyes to observe "inner space" for a few minutes a few times a day.

- ~ Eat a morsel of food with your eyes closed. Chew slowly to truly appreciate the taste and the texture.

- ~ Go outside. Take a slow, mindful walk. Immerse yourself in Nature with no distractions.

Dharana "OMwork"

- ~ Close your eyes and imagine a time when you were able to connect on a profound level with something or someone to the point that time seemed to stand still. How did you feel?

- ~ **In a conversation, be a good listener.** Can you connect on a level that is deep enough that you may truly feel what the person is saying?

Dhyana "OMwork"

- ~ Practice sitting meditation for five minutes per day for one week.

- ~ Practice sitting meditation for ten minutes per day for the second week.

- ~ Practicing walking meditation.

- ~ Research metta meditation, or loving-kindness meditation. Record some metta phrases, or implement a suggested metta practice. The following link offers some insight: http://info.med.yale.edu/psych/3s/metta.html

- ~ Eat a whole meal slowly and silently.

CHAPTER
6

Getting Started

ronfromyork/Shutterstock.com

"The journey of a thousand miles begins with a single step."

—Lao Tzu, *The Tao Te Ching*

 Materials Needed for Each Class

- A yoga mat (please consider an eco-friendly mat)
- A hand towel if you sweat a lot
- Comfortable clothing (not too loose or baggy) that allows freedom of movement but won't get in the way
- An old scarf or yoga strap (if you have steel hamstrings)
- A pen or pencil
- A folder, journal, or binder with some lined paper if you will be choosing not to write directly in this text/workbook

In our consumer-driven, capitalist society, you might believe that yoga is a commodity. While the above items will help you to be more comfortable in class as you learn the practice, the reality is nothing is *really* needed with the exception of willful effort—which, as you know, cannot be bought.

What to Expect

As you begin the practice of yoga, you can expect some initial muscle soreness. This should be mild and should lessen within the first few weeks. When you start to increase practice time through the semester, soreness will occur only when we add new postures that may target different muscles. Please remember that intense muscle soreness is a sign that you have pushed too far and have actually done some damage. To push *that* hard is a violation of all five yamas, the first limb of yoga.

In addition to mild soreness, it also is quite common to feel impatient, frustrated, and, at times, a little angry. The physical practice, as well as the deeper expressions of Yoga can be quite humbling. Through observation and svadhaya (self-study), a niyama within the second limb of yoga, you will learn so much about yourself. Remember: This was a practice designed to destroy what the ancient yogis referred to as the "lower nature," or ego. We are going for ego stripping, not ego building.

Enjoy the awareness you will be creating. Watch the emotions come up, honor each, and then without attachment, go back to the breath. Do this all as if you were seeing through a new lens. You will soon discover that you are *way bigger* than your thoughts.

A strong emotion occasionally may rise all the way to the surface. It may feel as if you want to laugh or cry uncontrollably. This can be unsettling. Most people don't know what to do when this occurs. Go *with* it, not against it. Cry. Laugh. Let the prana (energy) *move!* This is a phenomenon that can arise when an area of blocked energy inside the body, or granthi, has been reopened. Blockages in the nadis, or energy pathways, are believed to be created by physical or emotional "scarring", or samskaras. Physical injury and surgical procedures can undeniably cause scar tissue in the body, but what about emotional scarring? Anyone who has had a granthi opening happen during yoga practice will tell you how powerful this is and how amazing the release it brings can be.

Preparing for Practice

Before we go any further, both journaling and the concept of setting an intention for each practice period warrant consideration. We will be doing both throughout the semester. Journal pages are shaded and can be found at the back of this book.

Journaling

When you enter the classroom, please take a couple of minutes to record how you feel prior to practice. This can be as simple as a few words or as elaborate as a diary entry. It is up to you. You will be the only one, if you wish, who will see these journals. Then at the end of each class, ask yourself again how you feel.

As the semester progresses, you will be able to observe patterns from what you've written—these patterns will help you make adjustments if necessary. For instance, if you notice that you are always tired in the morning, perhaps you will need to allow yourself more time to sleep in the evenings.

Adjusting your schedule to allow this extra sleep time will be another step toward wellness. You likely already knew that you need more sleep—but seeing on paper the effect of your late nights as manifested by the body can be a compelling motivation.

Maybe the foods you are eating (or not eating) are creating this feeling of lethargy. Maybe you are getting too much sleep. No matter what the cause of your symptoms, it is helpful to see this on paper. Other patterns may emerge from this pre- and postclass journaling. As is the case in much, if not all, of the time, you will notice feeling better after a mindful practice.

Setting an Intention

The Sanskrit word for intention is *sankalpa*. It can also be translated as will, resolution, purpose, or "the heart's desire."

When you step to the edge of your mat, ready to begin each practice session, it is essential to understand why you are doing so. You are giving yourself the opportunity to show up for yourself—to pay attention. Students sometimes have shared their intentions with their class. Here are some that are memorable:

- I intend to feel better.
- I intend to create more energy.
- I want an A in this class.
- I want to wake up for my next class today.
- I want to stretch my hamstrings.
- I want to forgive my roommate (or another significant person).
- I want to sweat!
- I want to get out of my head for a while.
- I want clarity.
- I intend for my back to feel better.
- I want to loosen up before (or after) football (or another sport) practice.
- I want to relax.
- I intend to create Yoga.

So, every time you roll out your mat to practice, ask yourself:

- Why *am* I practicing?
- What do I need today?
- What do I intend to create from this practice?

Do your best to keep ego out of your intention. For example, "I want nice abs" or "I want toned arms" would be ego-based intentions. You may very likely end up with those things, but allowing yourself to explore the beauty of the bigger picture will allow you to view yourself with more clarity and compassion.

What makes an intention different from a goal?

Goal setting can be incredibly helpful in achieving and maintaining success in certain areas, but often we set goals that are unrealistic, unattainable in the time period allowed, and sometimes difficult to measure. A good thing to remember as you embark on a yoga practice is that most successes are dependent on the numerous "failures" that preceded it! The great thing is that practicing yoga in the spirit with which yoga was intended allows you to see clearly that there really is no failure. Everything is a lesson. You learn the lesson and move on, or you continue to repeat it over and over.

Consider intention setting to be your ability to create an energy field you willingly step into in order for that sankalpa to manifest.

Please ask questions before, during, or after practice. Many times your classmates are grateful to have an answer to something they too were wondering about. From the middle to end of the semester, questions should be asked either before or after class to ensure we are keeping focus through the physical practice.

General Guidelines

Below are some guidelines that should help you create awareness and steadiness through the physical practice in order to create a strong practice.

Before Class Begins

- *Hydrate!* Drink at least ten to twenty ounces of water an hour or more before class. You will sweat. Eventually, the practice may leave you drenched. Many people come to this style of yoga because of the purifying effect it has. Please leave your water bottle with your belongings. You should not have to take water breaks if you hydrated properly ahead of time. A break in practice is distracting to you and to others.

- A light meal three to four hours prior to class or a light snack one to two hours prior is acceptable. Asana is best practiced on a *fairly* empty stomach. That said, please do *not* come in famished.

- Avoid caffeine prior to practice.

- Do not smoke prior to class. You may not smell it, but everyone else does.

- Use proper hygiene.

- Be prepared to go barefoot for practice. Please wear socks with treading if you have any foot condition requiring your feet to be covered.

- Avoid lotions, potions, and perfumes. A scent you like may have chemicals or properties that cause an allergic reaction in someone else. Lotions will make your hands and feet slippery and will not allow you to sweat properly. Your skin is the largest organ of your body. Be kind to it.

- Remove any jewelry that hinders movement and focus.

- Unless you are the President of the United States of America, a doctor or nurse on call, your wife is nine months pregnant, or you have an *urgent* family issue, turn your Weapons of Mass Distraction, otherwise known as cell phones, to vibrate and leave with your belongings. If any of the above situations apply to you, please put your phone on vibrate near your mat and leave the room when you get your call.

- Please inform your instructor of any medical conditions that may hinder your ability to do yoga postures. This will help the instructor to give you specific modifications, allowing you to create a practice suitable for your needs.

- Arrive on time! Please remove shoes and place out of the way with any other items you don't need for class.

- Set an intention for each practice.

During Class

- Allow these three focal points (Ashtanga essentials) to direct your practice:

    1. Breath: Breathe deeply

    2. Bandhas: (specific muscle locks)

    3. Drishti (gazing points): Smile softly

- Listen with love, respect, and compassion to the messages your body gives you. Your body is an amazingly wise instrument.

- Please *do not talk!* This is annoying to your classmates, and it hinders self-awareness. At the end of each semester for the past 16 years, the most popular answer to the question: "What did you like the least about this class?" was that students talked during practice. Please consider the possibility that even if you took the class for fun, easy credits, perhaps everyone else took it to learn yoga. Besides, Patanjali said thousands of years ago that every time we open our mouths, prana (energy) gets out. You will need your prana.

- If it doesn't feel good, *it is not good*. The practice should be a challenge. It should not cause pain or suffering.

- Learn to find your "edge." Sometimes there is a fine line between working hard and pushing *too hard*—to the point of pain. Be mindful of that line, and do not cross it.

- Learn to distinguish between exhaustion and laziness. When you are feeling extremely tired, take your practice down a notch. If you are feeling lazy, turn it up a notch.

- Do not compete with anyone. This includes you. When you catch yourself thinking things like "I used to be able to do this" or "I should be able to do this like so-and-so" *stop* and breathe. Really *feel* the pose. Observe your emotions and back up. Nothing should ever hurt. Work 100% with 0% pain.

- Remember that someone mindfully breathing in a gentle pose (what we will call Plan A in class) is practicing yoga, but someone struggling to do a deeper expression of that pose (Plan C) is practicing...insanity!

Create BE-ing

We are called human *beings*, rather than human *doings*. In class there will undoubtedly be occasions when you feel as if you would rather be doing something else, like sleeping in, or watching the big game, or going out with friends. Witness this impatience and pull yourself back to the simplicity of what you are trying to create: union. As a matter of fact, *any* time you catch yourself thinking that you would rather be sleeping or fishing or at the beach or anything other than what is going on right here and now, take a deep breath and re*mind* (a great word, really) yourself that you can really only *BE* right where you are.

Search your heart and see, the way to do is to be.

—*Lao Tzu, The Tao Te Ching*

Pick a Plan

Different "plans" for the postures will be offered in class. For example, a forward bend may look like this:

Plan A:

And a Plan B would look like this:

Or Plan C:

When appropriate, options will be shown for the posture done from a chair:

Plan A:

Plan B:

Practiced with awareness, Hatha yoga will help you build strength and flexibility, among other qualities. Yoga postures done improperly, or without focus, can actually hurt more that help, so please avoid the ego-driven temptation to move into Plan B until Plan A feels easy. Generally, if you cannot breathe deeply and smile softly in a posture, it is the wrong one!

After Class

- Remember to check back with the intention you set for practice, and do post class journaling.

 Ashtanga Essentials

1. Breath
Creating the Perfect Breath for Asana Practice

Even though pranayama, the control of breath, is considered the fourth limb of yoga, it is appropriate to learn the basics ahead of time. A more in-depth exploration of pranayama can be found in Chapter 8.

The practice of the postures requires fuel. Along with adequate rest and good nutrition, your breath is your fuel.

According to the ancient texts, asana and pranayama are done together to purify the energy pathways, or nadis, in the body (Sivananda Vedanta Center, 2000). When energy is flowing freely; when we have created a balance in the body, the mind, and the spirit, it is believed that we will experience a state of wholeness. We will be well.

For asana practice, your pattern of breathing is essential in creating the perfect brain chemistry that will make it possible for you to do something incredibly physical while remaining calm. Refinement of a steady breath will eventually permit you to breathe in and out at the same rate, allowing the right and left hemispheres of the brain to work together.

Dirgha Pranayama: Three-part Control of Life Force

Visualize an empty glass. Now visualize water pouring into that glass. Watch it rise from the bottom to the middle, and then rise to the top of that glass. Now imagine the glass of water as it would empty if you were drinking it. "See" how it empties from the top to the middle, and lastly, all the way to the bottom? This is how you will be filling and emptying your lungs in dirgha pranayama. If this visualization does not work well, imagine your lungs as two balloons. "Watch" the balloons filling from the bottom to the middle to the top. Empty them in reverse: top, middle, bottom.

- On your back (with knees bent, if necessary), place your hands over your lower abdomen. Take a deep, slow breath in and feel your lower belly rise. Exhale and feel your belly fall. This is part 1 of the three-part breath. Repeat a few more times to really feel the movement of the diaphragm and abdomen.

- Now, move your hands up to your rib cage. Cross your arms and wrap hands and fingers around your rib cage so your shoulders will not become tense. Breathe in deeply, feeling your lower belly rise. Slowly move the breath up higher, feeling your rib cage expanding as the intercostals expand. This is part 2 of the three-part breath. Breathe out and feel the ribs drop and the belly drop as the lungs slowly (but never completely, thank goodness) deflate. Repeat until you can really feel the lungs filling from the bottom (part 1) to the middle (part 2) on the inhalation and the lungs emptying from the middle (part 2) to the bottom (part 1) on the exhalation.

- Last, move the hands to the chest, with elbows in toward the waist and the shoulders relaxed. Take a deep breath. Feel breath move from the bottom (part 1—belly rising) to the middle (part 2—ribs expanding) to the top (part 3—chest lifting). Try not to allow your face, neck, or shoulders to tense up as the breath moves upward. Feel the collarbone (right and left clavicular region) and the shoulders expand outward and slightly upward. Now exhale in reverse: 3—chest, 2—ribs, 1—lower belly.

Practice this breath. The great news is you can practice anywhere. No one will know. Try it while driving, while waiting for anything, while sitting in class or at work, while in the shower or bath, while in the middle of a conversation (the listening part, since almost all talking is done on an exhalation). Notice the difference. You will be able to stay attentive to the task at hand, whatever it is, while bringing balance to the body and mind.

Once you have an understanding of the three-part breath, it is time to move on to lengthening the breath. Breathing into quadrants (lower back, lower belly, collarbone and shoulder blades) will allow you to feel the multi-dimensional quality to deep breathing. Have no fear—all of this will get easier with each practice session.

On inhalation—

Part 1: Breathe in slowly—belly rises.

Part 2: Continue breathing in slowly—ribs expand.

Part 3: Continue a slow, steady inhale—chest lifts, collarbone and shoulders push upward and outward.

On exhalation—

Part 3: Breathe out slowly-chest falls, shoulders and collarbone sink.

Part 2: Continue breathing out slowly—ribs fall.

Part 1: Continue a slow, steady exhalation—belly will fall.

Try the following method to create samavritti, or same fluctuation, with the breath:

1. Create the three-part breath.

2. With a soft face and shoulders relaxed, begin to put a count (in your head) to the in-breath. Find a completely comfortable count that allows you to keep the face, neck, and shoulders relaxed.

3. Now match your out-breath to that same count, mindful that you are moving the breath completely. Keep this established ratio going, and notice a slight pause both before the in-breath and after the out-breath.

If you were able to bring the breath in to a count of 8, for instance, here is what the ratio may look like: 8 (inhale): 1 (pause): 8 (exhale): 1 (pause).

Keep in mind that breath is multidimensional. It does not just move up and down, like this:

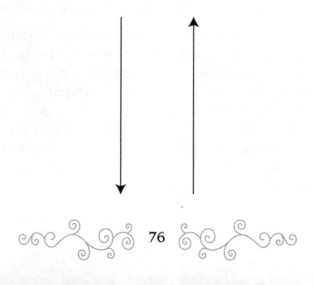

It is moving upward and outward, downward and inward. It is expanding and contracting. It is much like the ebb and flow of the ocean.

Try these visualizations when breathing:

© Kendall Hunt Publishing Company

Last, but not least, we will explore ujjayi pranayama, or victorious breath.

In *Beyond Power Yoga* (2000), Beryl Bender Birch encourages students to create ujjayi breathing by whispering a short sentence out loud, and then again with the mouth closed. When doing this, a contraction in the back of the throat (at the epiglottis) can be felt. These "whisper muscles" are what control a slow, steady flow of breath in and out. Try this when you are alone—otherwise, someone may think you are insane:

1. Whisper the word *yoga* (out loud) on an exhalation.

2. Inhale deeply and do it again and again, lengthening it each time.

3. Whisper the word *yoga* on an inhalation.

4. Now make it one syllable only: "Yo" on the exhale and "ga" on the inhale

5. Lengthen both parts.

6. Make the sound "haaaaaaaaaaaaaa" on the exhale and "aaaaaaaaaaaaaahhh" on the inhale or "huuuummmmm" on the inhalation and" ssaaaaaaaaaaaaaaaa" on the exhalation.

7. Lengthen both parts.

8. Close your mouth and breathe this sound in and out, breathing completely and cultivating samavritti. THIS is ujjayi pranayama.

In time you will be able to refine this breath, which is often affectionately called "Darth Vader" breath, or ocean breathing. You will eventually gain remarkable control of the breath using specific muscle locks, or bandhas.

2. Bandhas

The first two bandhas below eventually are intended to be held throughout practice. It takes years of regular practice to refine them to the point that they can be held throughout. Be patient.

Bandhas are a series of internal energy gates within the subtle body that assist in the regulation of pranic flow. They three bandhas are mulabandha, uddiyana bandha, and jalandhara bandha. You may think of them as valves that work similarly to the valves within the circulatory system. When the heart beats, blood surges through arteries and veins. Valves keep the blood from sloshing back toward the heart. In this way, when the heart beats, the blood can continue its forward movement. Bandhas regulate the flow of prana (life force) in a similar way within subtle energy channels known as nadis. When engaging the locks, energy is forced to spread throughout these pathways. We are then able to assimilate this energy on a cellular level as the prana bathes and feeds our subtle body and balances the gross nervous system.

Mulabandha

Mulabandha is the root lock. It is so called because of its location at the base of our nerve tree, the spinal column. There is a difference of location for this bandha in males and in females. In males, the seat of mulabandha is the perineal muscle, which is located in front of the anus and behind the genitals. In females the location is near the top of the cervix. A good way to understand its location is to imagine that you have a need to go to the toilet and there is not one in sight. Which muscles would you use to resist this urge?

Uddiyana Bandha

The second lock is uddiyana bandha, which means "flying upward." In its complete expression, uddiyana bandha is performed by exhaling fully and then drawing the lower belly inward and upward while simultaneously lifting the diaphragm. This level of uddiyana bandha is primarily utilized during the exhale retention phase of specialized breath control methods known as pranayama. This full level of engagement is not possible to maintain throughout practice due to the inability to inhale while total uddiyana bandha is engaged. The level of uddiyana bandha we should hold for the duration of our practice is more subtle. Rather than sucking in the belly fully, we must instead simply maintain a stillness located three fingers below the navel. This will allow space for the diaphragm to drop during each inhale, and the lungs' expansion will find its way into the side ribs, back, and chest. The upper portions of the torso must remain soft and pliable so that the inhale expansion may occur to its fullest expression. Upon each exhale, the lower abdominal muscles may contract to encourage a total emptying of the lungs. This contraction must then be released for the inhale to repeat fully, yet not relaxed so much that the lower belly rises with the incoming breath. The action is subtle. Too much effort and the breath is hindered rather than enhanced.

Jalandhara Bandha

Jalandhara bandha is the third lock. It is the chin lock. This lock is not utilized as frequently as the other two. It occurs spontaneously in some asanas, such as Shoulderstand, and is prescribed for use in others. It is, however, used extensively for pranayama, which is addressed minimally in this text.

To engage jalandhara bandha, you may extend the chin forward and then draw it back into the notch that is formed where the two clavicles meet at the bony protrusions below your Adam's apple. When engaging all three bandhas simultaneously. it is called "mahabandha," or the great lock.

Bandhas are an integral part of Ashtanga yoga. As your personal practice develops, you will understand them more fully.

Drishti
"Looking out/looking in"

Drishti is a point of gaze, or focus, yet it has little to do with our physical sight. The real "looking" is directed internally. We may fix our physical sight upon an external object or a specific point on our body, yet truly the drishti is meant to direct our attention to the subtle aspects of our practice, which were discussed earlier: the breath and bandhas, as well as the mind.

Those of us with sight are easily distracted by our surroundings. Other students in the room, a clock on the wall, or myriad other forms may pull us away from the immediate concerns of practicing yoga with awareness. The drishti is a "device" designed to balance our internal and external practice.

In Ashtanga yoga, there are officially nine drishti points. They are listed below. If you find the drishtis to be too difficult, you may follow this general rule of thumb as an alternative when

necessary: Let your gaze move in the direction of the stretch. You may think of your eyes like a doll's eyes, which will follow the movement of your head. When the head moves, the gaze will follow in the same direction.

Remember, the main focus is to look inward. Create an internal checklist that you can scan in a millisecond while practicing. On this list you may have:

- Breath

- Bandhas

- Flow, or vinyasa; the linking of the breath and movement

- Equality of opposition; stretching in all directions from your center of gravity

- Awareness—where is it? Do you feel tension in particular areas of the body? Are you relaxed?

The list may go on, but the idea is that the drishti is your microscope to examine that which may not be seen externally.

Utilize the prescribed drishti (below) for each asana, or utilize the general rule of gazing in the direction of the stretch, as stated above.

1. Nasagrai: Tip of the nose

2. Ajna chakra: Between the eyebrows

3. Nabi chakra: Naval

4. Hastagrai: Hand

5. Padhayoragrai: Toes

6 and 7. Parsva drishti: Far to the right or far to the left

8. Angusta ma dyai: Thumbs

9. Urdhva or antara drishti: Up to the sky

Test Your Knowledge

Name _____ **Date** _____

1. Why is it important to set an intention for practice?

2. List five things you need to do before class to be prepared to practice.

3. What are the three main things you should focus on to direct your practice?

4. According to the ancient texts, why are asana and pranayama practiced together?

5. Summarize a three-part breath, or dirgha pranayama. Be specific.

6. What does the Sanskrit word *samavritti* mean?

7. What does the word *ujjayi* mean and how is ujjayi pranayama different than dirgha pranayama?

8. Name the three bandhas and briefly describe each.

9. What is the purpose of drishti?

Recommended titles to explore the concepts within this chapter:

Sri K. Pattabhi Jois. *Yoga Mala.* North Point Press, New York, NY, 2002

Gregor Maehle. *Ashtanga Yoga: Philosophy and Practice.* New World Library, Novato, CA, 2006

David Swenson. *Ashtanga Yoga: The Practice Manual: An Illustrated Guide to Personal Practice.* Ashtanga Yoga Productions, Austin, TX, 1999

Richard Freeman. *Yoga Breathing.* Audio book: Sounds True, Inc., Louisville, CO, 2002

B.K.S Iyengar. *Light on Pranayama: The Yogic Art of Breathing.* The Crossroad Publishing Co, New York, NY, 1981

B.K.S Iyengar. *Light on Life.* Rodale, Emmaus, PA, 2005

Donna Farhi. *The Breathing Book: Vitality & Good Health Through Essential Breath Work.* Henry Holt & Co. New York, NY, 1996

Swami Buddhananda. *Moola Bandha: The Master Key.* Yoga Publications Trust Ganga Darshan, Munger, Bihar, India, 1978

Find some time to practice dirgha pranayama throughout the day.

Some tips to help you remember to practice:

- If you wear a watch, switch it to the other wrist for a week or so. Every time you check the time, it will be a reminder to breathe deeply.

- Wear a wristband of some sort if you do not typically wear one.

- Put sticky notes in conspicuous places that say *"breathe."*

- Make it a point to breathe this way when listening to someone speak.

Once you have begun to consistently do well with this:

Find a time each day when you are alone to practice ujjayi breathing. Cultivate this breath with some basic movement. For example:

Standing tall with arms by sides, begin to lift arms up and over your head on an inhalation. Return arms by your sides on an exhalation. Slow the movement as you learn to control and slow the breath.

7 Your Practice: A Fifteen-Week Practice Based on Ashtanga Vinyasa Yoga

The Guest House

This being human is a guest house.
Every morning a new arrival.

A joy, a depression, a meanness,
some momentary awareness comes
as an unexpected visitor.

Welcome and entertain them all!
Even if they're a crowd of sorrows,
who violently sweep your house
empty of its furniture,
still, treat each guest honorably.
He may be clearing you out
for some new delight.

The dark thought, the shame, the malice,
meet them at the door laughing,
and invite them in.

Be grateful for whoever comes,
because each has been sent
as a guide from beyond.

—Rumi

Yoga pose photos in this chapter courtesy of Rachel Donley.

Asana Practice

For *every* asana practice, you will be asked to:

1. Roll out the mat (the "welcome mat" to your "guest house"), making sure alignment provides sufficient space to move fully.

2. Go to the Journal pages to note how you feel prior to practice and to set an intention for practice.

3. Stand at the top of the mat to create awareness, cultivate proper breathing, and review intention.

4. Complete (most days) a thirty to sixty-minute asana practice. Listen to your body and heed any modifications for positions that are not advisable (contraindicated) for any conditions you may have.

5. Take a five to ten-minute relaxation. This will occasionally be followed by a seated meditation period.

6. Complete a post class journal.

General rules for each asana:

~ Breathe deeply.

~ Smile softly.

~ Engage bandhas.

~ Maintain soft gaze (drishti).

~ Take five deep breaths per posture.

~ Feel each asana extend in every direction from your center of gravity.

~ Use the inhalation to lengthen and the exhalation to extend deeper in the posture.

~ Use the muscles needed to be in the posture, and try to let go of what is not needed, especially in the shoulders, neck, and face.

~ In many asanas, your shoulder blades (scapulas) will be stabilized by engaging the muscles needed to keep them held in to the back of the rib cage. This scapular stabilization is the perfect anecdote to all the daily forward bending from texting and computer time.

The First Three Weeks of Practice

The following aspects of practice will be covered:

Week 1

• Three-part breathing (dirgha pranayama) and quadrant breathing

• Basic postures of Sun Salutation A and B (surya namaskara A and B)

• Fitness assessment (page 155)

- Stress assessment (page 161)
- Relaxation (savasana)

Week 2

- Review of three-part breathing (dirgha pranayama) and quadrant breathing
- Samavritti (same fluctuation breathing)
- Victorious Breathing (ujjayi pranayama)
- Review Sun Salutation A
- Sun Salutation B (surya namaskara B)
- Relaxation

Week 3

- Review of dirgha pranayama, samavritti, and ujjayi pranayama
- Review Sun Salutations A and B
- Begin learning Standing Sequence Postures (page 94)
- Begin learning Primary Series Postures (page 104)
- Begin learning Closing Sequence Postures (page 114)
- Relaxation

Basic Asanas of the Sun Salutations (Surya Namaskara A and B)

- **Equal Standing** (samasthiti)   *Drishti (gazing point): The "horizon"

Stand at the front of your mat with big toes touching and heels apart slightly. Spread your toes to the best of your ability. Feel your weight distributed equally in your feet. Imagine a gentle lift from the arches of your feet and from the kneecaps. Feel the spine lengthening, with arms by your sides and heart lifted. Create a feeling of lifting through the entire body.

From a chair (for foot or leg injuries)   Sit with feet hip width apart.

- **Upward Stretch** (urdhva uttanasana)   *Drishti(s): Horizon to thumbs

Plan A (for tight shoulders)   From samasthiti, rotate palms upward as you begin to raise the arms to the side. Take arms as far up as comfortable.

Plan B   From samasthiti, rotate palms upward as you begin to raise the arms to the side and overhead. Upper arms will be in front of the ears. Press hands lightly while looking Up to the thumbs. Keep length in the neck. Keep face soft and breath smooth and steady to sync with the movement.

From a chair   With feet hip width apart following directions above.

- **Forward Bend** (uttanasana)   *Drishti(s): Horizon to shins (eventually tip of the nose)

Plan A   Fold forward with knees bent and arms stretching to the sides. Place hands to the thighs and press belly, ribs, and chest to the legs. Let the neck lengthen. Use the thighs to help to support the back as you fold forward, and place hands to floor, if possible.

Plan B   Same as A with legs straighter and hands coming directly to the floor.

Plan C   Same as B but with legs as straight as possible. Engage quadriceps.

From a chair   With feet hip width apart, following directions above.

- **Half Forward Bend** (ardha uttanasana)   *Drishti: Horizon (eventually tip of the nose)

Plan A From Forward Bend, lift and lengthen the spine with knees bent. Use your hands on your thighs to help to support the back as you lift up if you have low back problems.

Plan B Same as A with legs straight and hands to the floor. To prevent the cervical spine from being compromised (as in photos below), please elongate the neck and use your eye muscles to gaze forward while able to keep a long neck.

From a chair The same as A.

- **Plank** Drishti: *Horizon (eventually tip of the nose)

Plan A   A push-up position with hands directly under shoulders and knees touching the floor. To lower down, tip slightly forward to bring some weight into the fingertips. Drop the knees gently down and lower from hips to belly and then chest, keeping the back as straight as possible.

Plan B   A plank position with elbows bending straight back and over the wrists (chaturanga dandasana). Spine long, shoulders pushing gently back, away from the ears. Lift the heart and lower to the belly.

Plan C   Same as B without lowering to the floor. Remain in chaturanga dandasana to lift directly to upward facing dog.

- **Cobra** (bujangasana) *or* **Upward Dog** (urdhva mukha svanasana)   *Drishti: Horizon to ceiling (eventually to the tip of the nose)

Plan A (modified Cobra)   With forearms down and in tight to the body, and elbows near the waist. Lift the heart, gently pressing forearms down to create a gentle press of the shoulders downward. Shoulder blades go in and down the back of the ribs to open the chest.

Plan B (Cobra)   Same as A with hands directly under the shoulders to lift and open the chest.

Plan C Upward Dog (adho mukha svanasana):   Same as B with knees off the floor, toes pointed, and quadriceps firm.

From a chair   From Half Forward Bend, reach back to softly grasp the sides of the chair. Lift the heart, stretching the arms and chest.

- **Child's Pose** (balasana)   *Drishti: Between the knees

Plan A   From all fours, sink the buttocks down over the heels and rest head on hands.

Plan B   Same as A with buttocks resting on heels and head on floor arms stretched forward.

- **Downward Dog** (adho mukha svanasana)　*Drishti: Between the knees

Plan A　Child's Pose.

Plan B　From all fours, spread your palms, fingers, and thumbs, and turn toes under. With knees bent and heels lifted, extend the hips as high upward and backward as comfortable. Firm the outer thighs and roll the inner thighs slightly outward. Press the "roots" of the fingers and thumbs into the floor to firm the outer arms, allowing a slight "scooping" of the inside of the elbows to protect the shoulders. Feel your shoulder blades being drawn toward the tailbone. Head should remain between the upper arms, with neck long. Distribute the effort evenly throughout the body. Stability should be felt in hands, feet, and core.

Plan C　Same as B with legs straight and heels drawn down to the floor.

- **Fierce Pose** (utkatasana)   *Drishti: Horizon to thumbs

Same as Equal standing to upward facing stretch with the exception of a bend in the knees. Back should be elongated, abdominals engaged, and weight distributed evenly in the feet.

- **Warrior I** (virabhadrasana A)   *Drishti: Thumbs (except in A)

Plan A   Stand with feet apart at least the length of your legs. Spread the toes and place one foot forward and the back foot turned in about 45 degrees. Place hands on hips, relax shoulders, soften face, and look to the horizon. Bend the front knee to 90 degrees, directly over ankle. Do not let the knee dip inward. Align the outer edge of the kneecap with the outer edge of the foot. Press down through the back edge of the back foot. Lift from the pelvic floor and distribute the effort throughout the pose, with the exception of keeping the face, neck and shoulders soft.

Plan B Same as A except arms and drishti. Begin to lift arms overhead. Stop them when you can longer lift without discomfort in the neck or shoulders. Look to the thumbs.

Plan C Same as B, with the exception of the arms. Lift the arms all the way overhead to press hands lightly together and look to the thumbs. Do not box the head in and keep the neck long. Face should be soft so breath can be deep and steady.

*Special note: Most of the drishtis offered in this section are for beginner students.

Surya Namaskara A (Sun Salutation A)

1. In **Equal Standing** (samasthiti), arms by sides.
2. From **Equal Standing** (samasthiti) inhale arms up.
3. Exhale and fold to **Forward Bend** (uttanasana).
4. Inhale and lift torso to **Half Forward Bend** (ardha uttanasana).
5. Exhale and walk (Plan A), jump (Plan B), or float (Plan C) back to **Plank** then lower to belly (Plan A) *or* go to chaturanga dandasana (Plan B or C).
6. Inhale to **Cobra or Upward Dog**.
7. Exhale and remain in **Child's Pose** *or* **Downward Dog** for five breaths.
8. Inhale to walk, jump, or float feet in to:
9. **Half Forward Bend** (ardha uttanasana).
10. Exhale and fold to **Forward Bend** (uttanasana).
11. Inhale to **Upward Stretch** (urdhva uttanasana).
12. Exhale to **Equal Standing** (samasthiti).

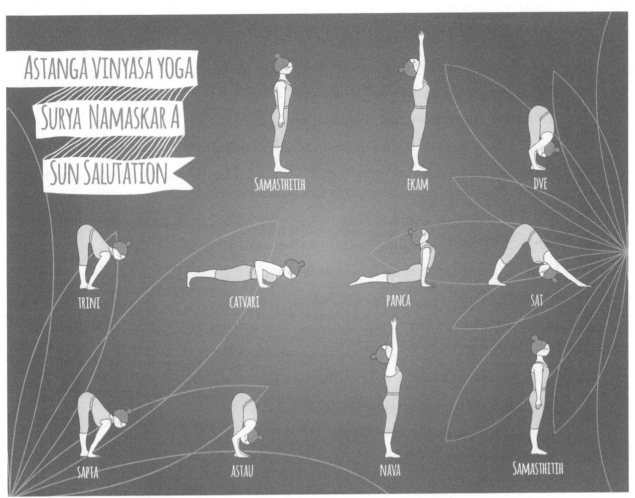

Semenova Mariia/Shutterstock.com

🪷 Surya Namaskara B (Sun Salutation B)

1. From **Equal Standing** (samasthiti), bend knees to:

2. **Fierce Pose** (utkatasana), and inhale arms around and up.

3. Exhale and fold to **Forward Bend** (uttanasana).

4. Inhale and lift to **Half Forward Bend** (ardha uttanasana).

5. Exhale and walk (Plan A), jump (Plan B), or float (Plan C) back to **Plank** then lower to belly (Plan A) *or* go to chaturanga dandasana (Plan B or C).

6. Inhale to **Cobra or Upward Dog**.

7. Exhale to **all four's, Child's Pose**, or **Downward Dog**.

8. Inhale to place right foot forward to **Warrior I**.

9. Exhale to **Plank** or chaturanga dandasana.

10. Inhale to **Cobra or Upward Dog**.

11. Exhale to **all four's, Child's Pose**, or **Downward Dog**.

12. Inhale to place left foot forward to **Warrior I**.

13. Exhale to **Plank** or chaturanga dandasana.

14. Inhale to **Cobra or Upward Dog**.

15. Exhale and remain in **Child's Pose or Downward Dog** for five breaths.

16. Inhale as you walk, jump, or float to **Half Forward Bend**.

17. Exhale and fold to **Forward Bend** (uttanasana).

18. Bend knees to **Fierce Pose** (utkatasana), and inhale arms around and up.

19. Exhale to **Equal Standing** (samasthiti).

Astanga Vinyasa Yoga
Surya Namaskar B
Sun Salutation

Samasthitih   Ekam   Dve   Trini   Catvari

Panca   Sat   Sapta   Ashtau   Nava   Dasa

Ekadasa   Dvadasa   Trayodasa   Chaturdasa   Panchadasa   Sodasa   Saptadasa   Samasthitih

Semenova Mariia/Shutterstock.com

🪷 Surya Namaskara A and B from a Chair

Surya Namaskara A

1. From seated: Place feet hip width apart and inhale arms overhead. Hands press lightly.
2. Exhale and fold to Forward Bend with hands on thighs.
3. Inhale and lift halfway up pushing with hands.
4. Exhale and reach back to gently grasp sides of chair.
5. Inhale to arch back and look up (Cobra).
6. Exhale to place hands back to thighs, fold, and remain for five breaths.
7. Inhale and lift halfway up, pushing with hands.
8. Exhale and fold to Forward Bend.
9. Inhale all the way up.
10. Exhale to arms by sides with feet hip width apart.

Surya Namaskara B

1. From seated: Place feet hip width apart and inhale arms overhead. Hands press lightly.
2. Exhale and fold to Forward Bend with hands on thighs.
3. Inhale and lift halfway up, pushing with hands.
4. Exhale and reach back to gently grasp sides of chair.
5. Inhale to arch back and look up (Cobra).
6. Exhale and turn to the right. Place right foot forward and left leg back into Warrior position.
7. Inhale to Warrior I.
8. Exhale to return to a forward position. Reach back to gently grasp sides of chair.
9. Inhale to Cobra.
10. Exhale and fold to Forward Bend with hands on thighs.
11. Inhale and lift halfway up, pushing with hands, if necessary.
12. Exhale and turn to the left for Warrior I.
13. Inhale to Warrior I.
14. Exhale to return to a forward position. Reach back to gently grasp sides of chair.
15. Inhale to Cobra.
16. Exhale and fold to Forward Bend with hands on thighs. Remain for five breaths.
17. Inhale and lift arms overhead with spine long. Push with hands, if necessary.
18. Exhale arms by sides with feet hip width apart.

A mind that is fast is sick.
A mind that is slow is sound.
A mind that is still is divine.

—Meher Baba
The Mantram Handbook

Consider the word *relax*. The word implies that we know, or at least remember, how to experience the ability to be lax (careless or laid back) in the first place. Some of you may be quite good at this. Most people are not. At least at first…

In Sanskrit, the word *savasana* means Corpse Pose. It symbolizes the end, or death, of your practice cycle. It is the practice of letting go. We let go of muscle locks and controlled breathing to let the breath take on a comfortable, natural rhythm. As your muscles relax, your breath, too, will relax. The breath will get very quiet and smooth. Without the need to control the breath, you can observe it as a means to stay present. Thoughts will come and thoughts will go. Do your best to try not to get too attached to the thinking. Settle in to a deep awareness of the here and now by returning to the breath when your thoughts are swinging wildly around. Many yoga practitioners refer to this wildly swinging mind as "monkey mind".

With eyes closed and breath slow and relaxed, you can observe both inner space, or all that is under your skin, and outer space, or all that available senses can explore outside your skin. Allow every cell of your body to bathe in the prana (energy) your practice was able to circulate. As stillness is experienced in the body, pure awareness will envelop you. Be patient. This does not happen in the first few practices, especially if you are a fast thinker.

It is essential that your back is comfortable during savasana. If bolsters are available, use one under your knees. If not, a backpack, rolled-up towel, or a coat can suffice.

🪷 Weeks Four through Nine

The teacher will determine the practice period necessary to cover the relevant concepts. Most asana practices will be twenty to forty-five minutes long. By weeks eight or nine, you may be ready to move into a forty-five-to sixty-minute practice.

At the beginning of each class, go to Journal pages and note the intention you have for practice today and how you are feeling before coming to your mat.

Standing at the top of your mat:

- Begin to cultivate awareness of breath, with hands to heart center.

- Create samavritti, and then ujjayi, if possible. Remind yourself that this breath, along with bandhas and drishtis, will guide you.

- Set your intention. On an exhalation bring arms by sides.

- Complete surya namaskar A two to three times and surya namaskar B two to three times.

- Practice two to five postures from Standing Sequence.

- Practice two to five postures from Primary Series.

- Practice two to five Closing Postures.

- Relax for five to ten minutes in savasana.

At the end of each class go back to Journal page to record post class assessment.

🪷 Standing Sequence Postures

The standing sequence is a laboratory to explore the physics of balance as understood on both the gross and subtle realms. Balance exists in the quality of opposition.

—David Swenson, from *Ashtanga Yoga "The Practice Manual"*

Courtesy of David Swenson.

We will learn *most* of the prescribed postures of the Standing Sequence. It takes years to refine these asanas. Most will be held for five breaths. Remember to allow your gaze to go in the direction of the stretch. As the semester progresses, we will explore the prescribed drishtis for the postures, as mentioned in the previous chapter, and suggested with each posture listed. Follow a plan that allows you to work hard, breathe deeply, smile softly, and experience no pain.

At the Completion of Surya Namaskara A and B, Step or Jump Feet Hip Width Apart to:

- **Forward Bend 1: "Foot Big Toe Posture"—Padangusthasana (Drishti: Tip of nose)**

Hands on hips. Inhale and left chest to look up, exhale, lead with the heart, and fold to:

Plan A   Hands on shins. Inhale to lift and lengthen the spine, exhale, and fold forward with knees bent. Elbows bend to the sides.

Plan B   Take toes. Inhale to lift and lengthen the spine. Exhale and fold with knees bent and elbows bent to the sides.

Plan C Same as B with legs straight.

Chair From seated: same as A or B.

Remain for five breaths. Inhale and lift up to half-forward bend. Place hands to hips (or push from thighs) and lift chest upward. Exhale as you step or jump feet together to samasthiti. Inhale as you step wide and to the right. Turn right toes out ninety degrees and left toes in about forty-five degrees for:

- **Extended Triangle Posture—Uttitha Ttrikonasana Right and Left (Drishti: Toes or hand)**

Plan A Slightly bent right knee, left hand to left hip. Lift heart and lengthen the spine. Look upward.

Plan B Same as plan A with both legs straight, a deeper stretch, and left arm extended to ceiling. Look to the left thumb.

Plan C   Same as plan B, with an even deeper stretch.

Chair   From seated: Same as A or B.

Turn right toes in to forty-five degrees and left toes out to ninety degrees to repeat asana on the left.

After completion of left side, turn the left toes in (to forty-five degrees) and right toes out (to ninety degrees) and turn to the right for:

- **Revolved Triangle Posture—Parivritta Trikonasana R, L (Drishti: Toes or hand)**

Plan A   Place right hand to right hip, and left hand to right shin. Elongate spine and twist to the right. Bend the right knee slightly. Look to the right.

Plan B   Same as plan A except: both legs are straight, right arm extends upward, left arm goes lower down left leg, and right thumb is the drishti.

Plan C   Same as plan B except: the left hand goes to the floor on the right side of the right foot. This is a deep twist!

Chair   Seated twist.

Turn right toes in (forty-five degrees) and left toes out (to 90 degrees) and turn to the left to repeat asana on the left.

After completion of left side, open to standing straddle, look left and turn left toes to step back to samasthiti (front of the mat). Inhale as you step and turn wide and to the right. Exhale into:

- **Extended Side Angle Posture—Utthitta Parsvakonasana Right and Left (Drishti: Hand)**

Plan A   Bend your right knee ninety degrees. Place your right forearm on right mid-thigh and left hand on left hip. Lift the heart, lengthen the spine, and rotate rib cage upward. Look upward in the direction of the stretch.

Plan B   same as plan A except: the left arm stretches up and over.

Plan C   same as plan B except: the right hand goes to the floor to the right side of the right foot. Left arm should be by the left temple.

Chair   From seated: same as plan A or B.

Turn right toes in (forty-five degrees) and left toes out (ninety degrees) and turn to the left to repeat asana on the left.

After completion of left side, turn L toes in (forty-five degrees) and R toes out (ninety degrees) and turn to the right for:

- **Revolved Side Angle Posture—Parivritta Parsvakonasana (Drishti: Upward or hand)**

Plan A   Bend your right knee ninety degrees. Twist torso to the right to place left forearm on right mid-thigh and right hand on right hip. Lift the heart, lengthen the spine, and rotate rib cage to the right. Look to the right.

Plan B   Same as plan A except: the left elbow goes to the right side of the right (bent) knee. Right hand presses down on left hand to aid the twist to the right. Hands are in a prayer position.

Plan C   Left hand goes to the floor on the right side of the right foot. Right arm stretches up and over bring the upper arm by the right temple.

Chair   From seated: same as plan A or B.

Turn right toes in (forty-five degrees) and left toes out (ninety degrees) and turn to the left to repeat asana on the left.

After completion of left side, step back to samasthiti (front of the mat). Inhale as you step and turn wide and to the right to a standing straddle position. Exhale and place hands to hips. Inhale and lift heart to look up, exhale into:

- **Spread-Out Foot Posture A—Prasarita Padottanasana A (Drishti: Tip of nose)**

Plan A   Place hands to shins, bend knees, elongate the spine and fold to half forward bend.

Plan B   Keeping knees bent, place hands to floor (shoulder-width apart). Lift and lengthen the spine, and fold as far as comfortable, bending the elbows straight back to ninety degrees, if possible. Chin tucked in so that the neck is long, and head is in line with the spine. Look back at a point on the floor or to the tip of the nose.

Plan C   Same as plan B with both legs straight.

Chair   From seated: same as plan A.

Exhale and place hands to hips. Inhale and lift heart and torso to look up, exhale into:

- **Spread-Out Foot Posture B—Prasarita Padottanasana B (Drishti: Tip of nose)**

Hands stay on hips.

Plan A   Bend knees, elongate the spine and fold to half forward bend. Make sure the head stays in line with the spine.

Plan B   Same as plan A with legs straighter, and a deeper fold forward.

Plan C   Same as plan B with both legs straight.

Chair   From seated: same as plan A.

With hands remaining on hips, inhale and lift heart to look up, exhale to look forward and bring arms by sides. Inhale arms to a "T," exhale, and clasp hands behind back (or place knuckles to sacrum for Plan A). Inhale and lift to open the heart, exhale, and fold to:

- **Spread-Out Foot Posture C—Prasarita Padottanasana C (Drishti: Tip of nose)**

Plan A   Bend knees, elongate the spine and fold to half forward bend. Make sure the head stays in line with the spine. Keep knuckles on the sacrum.

Plan B   Same as plan A with legs straighter, and a deeper fold forward hands clasped (if possible) and pulling away from the low back to open the chest. Please keep scapulas stabilized by squeezing sliding them in and down along the back of the rib cage.

Plan C   Same as plan B with both legs straight, a deeper fold forward, and arms pulling up and over the head.

Chair   From seated: same as plan A.

   Inhale and lift heart to look up, exhale arms by sides. Inhale arms to a "T," exhale, and bring hands to hips. Inhale and lift to open the heart, exhale, and fold to:

- **Spread-Out Foot Posture D—Prasarita Padottanasana D (Drishti: tip of nose)**

Plan A   Place hands to shins, bend knees, elongate the spine and fold to half forward bend. Allow elbows to bend to the side.

Plan B   Keeping knees bent, place hands to floor. Hook toes if possible in "yogi toe lock". Lift and lengthen the spine, and fold as far as comfortable, bending the elbows out to the sides- to

ninety degrees, if possible. Chin tucked in so that the neck is long, and head is in line with the spine. Look back at a point on the floor or to the tip of the nose.

Plan C   Same as plan B with both legs straight.

Chair   From seated: same as plan A.

Place hands to hips. Inhale and lift heart to look up and come to standing. Exhale to look forward. Turn left toes to top of mat to step (or bend knees to jump) back to top of mat in samasthiti. Inhale as you jump or step to the right-feet apart about the length of your torso. Place hands in A—knuckles low back, B—knuckles mid-back, or C—reverse prayer position. Exhale and pivot ninety degrees to the right. Inhale and lift heart. Exhale and fold into:

- **Intense Side Stretch Posture—Parsvottanasana Right and Left (Drishti: Tip of nose)**

Plan A   Bend right knee slightly, elongate the spine and fold to half forward bend. Make sure the head stays in line with the spine. Keep knuckles on the sacrum and head in line with your spine. Push both sitting bones straight back as you pull the crown of the head straight ahead.

Plan B   Same as plan A with legs straighter, knuckles low-back (if possible), and a deeper fold forward.

Plan C   Deeper forward bend, placing chin to shin.

Chair   Sit and breathe.

Inhale and lift up to turn to left side to repeat. After left side, exhale to jump or step your feet to samasthiti.

- **Extended Hand to Big Toe Posture—Uutthita Hasta Padangusthasana Right and Left (Drishti: Straight ahead or toes)**

Plan A   Standing tall, place left hand on left hip and "bicep curl" the bent right knee as close to the belly and chest as possible. Look straight ahead. Remain here for five breaths. Open leg to the side for five breaths, keeping naval forward. Look over the left shoulder, if possible. Bring the leg back to the front, extend it forward and place both hands to hips for an additional five breaths. Relax your face, neck and shoulders. You cannot hold your leg up with your face, so don't waste your energy!

Plan B   Same as plan A with right leg straighter, and right hand to right foot in "yogi toe lock".

Plan C   Same as plan B with right leg straight. On the last part, lift leg upward to exhale and bring nose to knee before releasing leg to hold (hands back to hips) for the last five breaths.

Chair   From seated: same as A, B or C.

In the beginning, you may not be able to hold this posture for five breaths on each section. If necessary, only hold each part for three breaths until your build the muscular endurance to remain for five. After the right side is finished, repeat the whole sequence on the left. After left side is completed, take right leg up for:

- **Half-Bound Lotus Intense Stretch Posture—Ardha Baddha Padmottanasana Right and Left (Drishti: Straight ahead or toes)**

Plan A Place right foot below or above knee and open knee to the right for tree pose.

Plan B Take the right leg up as far as comfortable and drop the right knee to the right to open the glutes. Gaze straight ahead. Keep the spine long and the support leg straight.

Plan C Take the right leg to a half lotus.

Chair cross the right lower leg over the left leg, away from kneecap.

If the gluteals are too tight, cross the right leg at the lower left leg and fold slightly forward.

The full expression of this posture (Plan D) may be explored if there are students who are ready. After repeating posture on the left side, take a vinyasa; move through a sun salute A without holding in Downward Dog for five breaths. Walk, jump, or float feet forward to immediately lower buttocks to:

- **Fierce Posture—Utkatasana (Dristi: Straight ahead or thumbs) (from sun salute B)**

Plan A Hands on hips. Lift the heart, lengthen the low back and soften the face and shoulders.

Plan B With arms halfway up, rotate pinky fingers inward.

Plan C Arms in front of ears, look to thumbs.

Chair Same as A or B from seated.

Exhale and fold to Forward Bend. Lift to half forward bend. Step, jump, or float back to Plank or Chaturanga Dandasana. Move through Cobra or Up Dog, to Child's Pose or Down Dog. Place (from all fours) or step (from Down Dog) right foot forward for:

- **Warrior I—Virabhadrasana A Right and Left (Dristi: Straight ahead or thumbs) (from sun salute B)**

Plan A Bend right knee directly over ankle. Place hands on hips. Lift the heart, lengthen the low back and soften the face and shoulders. Press strong through the back leg. Look straight ahead.

Plan B Same as A with arms halfway up. Rotate pinky fingers inward if neck and shoulders feel tight. Lift the heart, lengthen the low back, and soften the face and shoulders. Look slightly upward.

Plan C Bring arms all the way up by ears and look to the thumbs with the hands pressing lightly together.

Chair Turn to the right ninety degrees. Same as A or B from seated.

Turn right toes in (forty-five degrees) and left toes out (ninety degrees). Turn to the left to repeat asana on the left. After completion of left side, open directly into next posture (Warrior II) over left foot first.

- **Warrior II Left - Right—Virabhadrasana B (Dristi: Straight ahead or hand)**

Plan A Keep the left knee bent directly over the ankle. Place hands on hips. Lift the heart, lengthen the low back and soften the face and shoulders. Fully engage the back leg by tightening your quadriceps. Look to the left, over the left shoulder.

Plan B   Same as A with arms halfway up, like a "T".

Chair   Same as A or B from seated.

Turn left toes in (forty-five degrees) and right toes out (ninety degrees). Turn to the right to repeat asana over the right leg.

Come out of Warrior II to take both hands to floor beside right foot. Step right foot back to Plank or lower to chaturanga dandasana. Take Cobra or Up Dog to Child's Pose or Down Dog. Come to a seated position for the beginning of the Primary Series.

The Primary Series Postures

In Sanskrit, Yoga Chikitsa means "yoga therapy." The Primary Series of Ashtanga yoga is designed to be therapeutic. It is intended as a means to cleanse and tone the body, mind, and spirit. As balance and alignment is restored in the musculoskeletal and nervous systems, energy can flow more freely in through the body. This ultimately allows all systems of the body to benefit. Most people notice a significant improvement in energy levels as well as increased mobility in the back, hips, chest, and the shoulders. We will explore only about half of the prescribed asanas of the Primary Series during the semester. As stated earlier in the purpose of this text, no disrespect is intended by the alteration of the traditional method of teaching the sequences to follow. Through many years of observation, the postures below were purposefully selected based on safety and general physical need for large class sizes of (mostly) college-aged students.

As in all asana practice, there are contraindications for each of these postures. Listen to the teacher regarding specific needs, and most of all, listen to your body.

Some Basic Postures of the Primary Series

- **Staff Posture—Dandasana (Drishti: Nose-chin down)**

Plan A From seated, with knees bent, press hands down beside hips to open the chest. Feel the shoulder blades squeezing gently together and sliding downward toward the tailbone. Ultimately, all three bandhas are engaged in this posture.

Plan B Same as plan A with straight legs extended forward and firm.

Inhale as you lift your heart and look up. Feel the sternum lifting and the spine lengthening. Exhale and fold to:

- **Seated Forward Bend, or Western Intense Stretch—Paschimottanasana A (Drishti: Toes)**

Plan A With legs straight, press arms into the floor to relieve pressure from the lower back. Fold forward to stretch the low back and hamstrings gently.

Plan B Same as A with knees bent, and hands placed on shins. Fold as deeply as comfortable.

Plan C   Take toes (yogi toe lock) and fold forward to lengthen the back.

There are two more Forward Bends to follow the asana above: paschimottanasana B (hands to sides of feet) and C (hands wrapped around feet). These may be investigated if there are enough students ready to do so.

Vinyasa: At this point in the practice, asanas will be linked with a series of movements that will be represented with the following symbol: **V**

There will be options (below) provided, but the key thing to remember is that if you *can* take one, *you really should*. This is a good time to remind yourself of your intention for practice and to contemplate whether you are really tired, or you are just being lazy.

The options for these vinyasas will be:

A: Sit, smile, breathe and wait.

B: (if wrists, elbows, or shoulders are bothering you) Sit and pull thighs into the belly keeping minimal pressure in the arms. Take a few breaths this way, pulling thighs to belly on the exhalation.

C: Inhale and press hands beside hips to lift buttocks off (or as close as possible to off) the floor. Exhale and lower. Inhale and come to an all fours. Exhale to step, jump, or float to Plank. Lower to the floor (knees down first, or like a push-up), or come to Chaturanga Dandasana. Inhale to Cobra, or Upward Facing Dog, exhale to Downward Facing Dog. Pull a knee forward, come gently to hip. Pull the other leg around to come to seated.

D: Inhale and press hands beside hips to lift buttocks off (or as close as possible to off) the floor. Exhale to push the legs through the arms to *either*:

- come to all fours to step, jump, or float to Plank (to lower to floor) or Chataranga Dandasana.
- jump or float immediately back to Plank or Chaturanga Dandasana.

Lift to Cobra or Up Dog on an inhalation, exhale to Down Dog. Bend knees to jump hips up high enough to feel some weight in your fingertips. Either cross at the shins to pull the legs through the arms to come to seated, or pull straight legs through to seated.

- **Head to Knee Pose—Janu Sirsasana A (Drishti: Toes): Right side to V to left side**

Plan A   Bend your right knee and let it drop gently to the right. Your legs should look like the letter "L". If this is not comfortable, place a rolled up towel (or extra mat) under the right hip or right knee. If you are *still* not comfortable, straighten the right leg into a straddle. Left knee can be bent slightly if it is too much for the hamstrings. Lift the heart and lengthen the spine. Only fold forward if it is comfortable.

Plan B   With no prop, create a slight bend in the left knee and fold half-way with hands to shins. Keep the heart lifted and the spine long.

Plan C   With left leg straight, take the left foot and fold forward.

V to:

- **Marichi's Pose A—Marichyasana A (Drishti: Toes): Right side to V to left side**

Plan A   Bend your right knee and place the right side of the right foot in line with the right side of the right hip. Left leg is bent to protect the hamstrings and low back, and is in line with the left hip. If this is not comfortable, elevate the hips. Lift the heart and lengthen the spine. The left arm pushes the spine long, as the right forearm pushes against the right shin to open the chest and shoulders.

Plan B   Same as A except: left leg is straight and right arm is wrapping around right leg to further open chest and shoulder. Wrap left arm around the back, if possible.

Plan C   Same as B with both arms wrapping and hands clasped. Left hand can take the right wrist, if it is possible to do so without pain or struggle. Fold forward, if comfortable.

<u>V</u> to:

- **Seated Twist—Marichi's Pose—Marichyasana C (Drishti: Over the shoulder): Twist to the right side to <u>V</u> to left side**

Plan A   Bend your right knee and place the right side of the right foot in line with the right side of the right hip. Left leg is bent slightly to protect the hamstrings and low back, and is in line with the left hip. If this is not comfortable, elevate the hips. Inhale to lift the heart and lengthen the spine. Exhale as the left arm wraps (mid-shin) around the right bent knee to aid in a gentle twist to the right. The right arm pushes the spine long.

Plan B   Same as A except: left leg is straight and left arm is wrapping around right leg to further open chest and shoulder. Twist to ninety degrees, if possible. Cross left arm over right leg, if you are able to twist to ninety degrees or more.

Plan C   Same as B with both arms wrapping and hands clasped behind the back. Right hand can take the left wrist, if it is possible to do so without pain or struggle. Twist as deeply as comfortable.

V to:

- **Boat Posture—Navasana (Drishti: Toes or tip of nose) Hold five breaths three to five times with lift off buttocks (or handstand!) in between each one**

Plan A   On floor with knees bent over the hips, lift the upper body up to engage the abdominals.

Plan B   Seated with knees bent. Hands under knees or arms extended midway. Keep the spine long.

Plan C   Same as B with legs and arms straight.

V to:

- **Bound Angle Posture—Baddha Konasana (Drishti: Nose, chin down)**

Plan A   Elevate the buttocks to relieve hip, knee, or back pressure, if necessary. Use arms to lengthen the low back. Lift heart to lengthen the spine. Gently press chin to chest.

Plan B   Sit tall with hands prying feet open like a book, and elbows in to your waist.

Plan C   Same as B with a forward bend.

V̲ to:

- **Seated Angle Posture—Upavishta Konasana (Drishti: In the direction of the stretch or to the third eye)**

Plan A Straddle with arms behind your back to relieve back pressure, if needed.

Plan B Straddle with hands to shins. Hinge from hips and fold forward.

Plan C Straddle with hands to feet. Hinge from hips and fold forward placing chin to floor.

V̲ to:

- Sleeping Big Toe Posture (Supta Pandangusthasana). This pose is the same as Standing Big Toe Posture in the Standing Sequence with the exception of being in a reclining posture. It is held five breaths with leg overhead, five with leg to the side, and five with the leg back overhead. There is no vinyasa in between sides.

Plan A   Lift into an abdominal contraction with your right knee bent, right hand to right leg and left hand to left thigh. Relax shoulders away from ears and keep the face soft. Hold for five breaths. Lower the head to the floor to take the right leg to the right. Look over your left shoulder. Hold for five breaths. Pull the right leg back overhead keeping the head resting on the floor for the last five breaths.

Plan B   Same as A with both legs straight, pulling the hamstrings to the most comfortable stretch.

After left leg lowers to the floor, rock up to **V**. Come into a reclining position to prepare for the Closing Postures. This is not the full sequence and is designed for student safety and the time span of the semester.

The final postures of the ashtanga yoga practice are challenging for many; eventually exhilarating for most. The modified section below will include two inversions. Inversions can be quite scary. Knowing your boundaries and respecting your body will be essential aspects in navigating this part of practice safely and mindfully.

When you were a baby, you most likely crawled before you stood up and walked before you learned how to run. Follow this approach and you will learn patience, persistence, and the ability to face your fears. When we safely confront our fear of something, we often develop enough self-confidence for those fears to disappear completely.

We will dissect the postures below in small segments. This will be done in five to ten minute chunks of time in a few classes. If you missed any of the instructional classes on inverting, you *may not* follow along. You may observe for a class period or two until you are ready. You cannot learn some of these postures *while* inverted!

The four mains systems of the body that are affected by inversions are the cardiovascular system, the lymphatic system, the nervous system, and the endocrine system. There are quite a few benefits of inverting for those who can do so safely. Most yoga teachers and students, as well as many health professionals, agree that inverting stimulates and regulates hormone production, improves the lymph system, strengthens the immune system, builds physical and emotional strength, and is a real boost for confidence. In addition, inverting naturally lowers blood pressure, giving the heart a break.

Inversions can be dangerous. Blood pressure can be affected significantly when we go against gravity. If you are unsure about inverting, consult your doctor. Know your blood pressure. If you have any of the contraindications below, please check with your doctor before attempting inversions. If you have none of the contraindications below, you will most likely be fine, but it is very important that you breathe deeply in an inversion so as not to create more pressure in the head and around the eyes.

Never Attempt an Inversion Alone

There are some key points to remember in your exploration of the Closing Postures:

1. Ask for help if you don't understand something or if you need assistance. We will be exploring these postures slowly by breaking them down in class. Since you will be on your back or inverted for most of the closing postures, you cannot learn the specifics without first observing them. If you missed any classes where these asanas were demonstrated and explained, please watch this section for a class period before attempting.

2. Contraindications: Do *not* invert if you have any of the following conditions:

    *   Hypertension—high blood pressure (not yet under control with medication)

    *   Hypotension—abnormally low blood pressure

- Orthostatic, or postural, hypotension—very low blood pressure
- Cervical spine problems
- Heart problems
- Epilepsy
- Eye pressure problems
- Reflux problems
- Pregnancy
- Headache that has not gotten better through practice

In most cases, the Plan A's suggested below will be suitable for the conditions listed above.

Some Basic Postures of the Closing Sequence

Most will be held for five breaths unless specified.

- **Bridge, or Upward Bow Posture—Urdhva Dhanurasana (Drishti: Straight ahead or nose)**

Plan A   From your back, press your arms by your sides and into the floor to lift the lower back up to a pelvic tilt. If your pectoral muscles (chest) are really tight, flip your palms upward here.

Plan B   Arms press straight down to open the chest. Inch the shoulder blades a little closer. Clasp hands if possible, and push the arms down to open the chest more deeply.

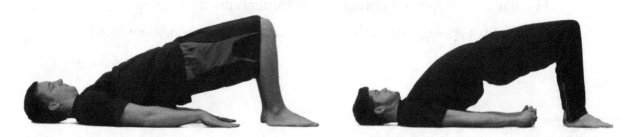

Plan C   Assisted backward bend.

Plan D   Full expression of the posture.

Rock up to V. Come to seated for:

- **Forward Bend—Paschimottanasana as described in Primary Series on page 78**

<u>**V**</u> **to come to reclining for:**

- **Shoulderstand—Salumba Sarvangasana (Drishti: Straight ahead or nose)**

Plan A   Rest on your back with knees bent, with or without support (block or bolster under your low back). Stay for ten to fifteen breaths with arms bent to the sides and palms up.

Plan B   Press arms into the floor to tip the hips to a half plough (described below). The weight should not be in your neck, but rather distributed between the shoulders and elbows. Support the low back with your hands. Stay for ten to fifteen breaths.

Plan C   Same as plan B except: the hands walk up the spine toward mid-back, allowing the legs to be lifted higher and more weight to be in the shoulder region. Stay out of your neck!

Lower both legs very slowly- mindful to stay away from the neck- to:

- **Half Plough or Plough—Ardha Halasana or Halasana (Drishti: Straight up or nose)**

Either posture you choose below is to be held for five to eight breaths. Lift the heart, and gently push shoulders down, away from the ears to keep the neck long. Lift the chin slightly away from the chest if there is too much of a stretch in the neck. Do not lift the head or look to the side.

With arms extended to the floor, roll out *slowly* along spine (top to bottom) to open into:

- **Fish Posture—Matsyasana (Dristi: In the direction of the stretch or nose)**

Plan A   From your back, with your head resting: begin to open the chest by pushing the arms down into the floor. Squeeze the shoulder blades together to lift the heart and open the rib cage. Do not push with the feet or lift the buttocks. Look to the ceiling.

Plan B   Same as A with a bend in the elbows to create a bigger chest opener. The back will arch enough that the head will naturally begin to drop back. Keep working hard with the arms to keep minimal weight in the head.

Plan C   Full expression: Full lotus, deep arch in the back/chest opener. Crown of the head on the floor. Tip of the nose is the drishti.

Come out of the posture after five to eight breaths to rock gently side to side before coming to seated for a <u>V</u> to an all fours to prepare for:

- **Headstand prep**

Once we begin working on this posture (likely mid-semester), we will work on adding a few extra breaths each week. This posture is to eventually be held for twenty-five breaths. We will do a maximum of fifteen only. Do not attempt a headstand on your own. This posture, done properly, should take months to years to learn-not one semester!

Step 1.   From all fours, drop gently for forearms to measure elbows to a shoulder width distance by wrapping fingers around upper arms, just above the elbows.

Step 2. Bring hands forward to clasp lightly without allowing elbows to spread wider than shoulder width. Push forearms into floor to engage the chest and shoulders. Let the neck release to look between the knees. This is Plan A.

Step 3. Tuck toes under. Push with forearms into the floor and begin to straighten the legs to tip the hips upward. This will be like a Downward Dog from the elbows. Let the head hang straight down. The head should *not* be touching the floor. This is Plan B.

- **Headstand prep—Sirsasana A (Drishti: Eventually to the nose)**

Plan A Photo above (Step 2). Stay five to ten breaths for two rounds.

Plan B With hips tipped upward, "walk" your feet in. Head should be hanging straight down and there should be minimal weight on the head. Hold for ten to twenty breaths.

Plan C Bend 1 knee, bringing that thigh in close to the belly and chest. Tip to hold (assisted) with the other foot to the floor. Once both thighs can be pulled, or tucked, into the belly (assisted) with no pressure on the head or neck, move to:

Plan D Full expression of the posture, against the wall—*assisted*.

When coming out of any of the postures described above, please lift the head *before* coming to the knees to protect your cervical spine.

Come down to rest in:

- **Child's Pose—Balasana (described on page 82)**

Come up to an all fours. <u>V</u> from knees to come to seated for:

- **Modified Lotus or Lotus—Padmasana (Drishti: Nose) Engage and all three locks**

Plan A No lotus. Sitting tall, using a prop to elevate hips, if needed, lift your heart and place hands over knees. Or put hands behind back, and push to the floor if necessary, to relieve back pressure.

Plan B Same as A with the right foot placed upon the left calf or upper thigh. Do not force this position. The hips need to be *really* open before this can be done without harm.

Plan C Full lotus. Same as B, with right foot on upper left thigh and left foot on upper right thigh.

After ten breaths, prepare for:

- **Scale Posture—Tolasana (Drishti: Up or nose)**

Plan A Fingertips down, thighs in tight. Hold the legs in with your core strength. Do not put pressure in the arms.

Plan B With hands down and hips up, allow knees to drop open to the sides.

Plan C Full expression. "Uprooting your lotus"

After ten to one hundred breaths, prepare for:

- **Savasana (as described on page 91)**

We will remain in savasana for five to ten minutes for most practice sessions.

Weeks Ten to Fifteen

The length of each practice period in weeks ten through fifteen will again be determined by the concepts and material the teacher may wish to share. Most practices will be forty-five to sixty minutes long. Post-testing for fitness and stress assessments will be completed between weeks thirteen and fifteen.

At the beginning of each class, go to Journal pages and note the intention you have for practice today and how you are feeling before coming to the top of your mat.

- Create awareness of breath, bandhas, and drishtis. Set intention.
- Surya namaskar A three to five times and surya namaskar B three to five times
- Five to eight postures from Standing Sequence
- Five to eight postures from Primary Series
- Five to eight Closing Postures
- Five to ten minutes in savasana
- Five to ten minutes in seated meditation

Go back to Journal page to record post class assessment.

 **A Gentle Approach**

On the days that a gentle practice seems more suitable, we will likely practice a number of the asanas suggested below. The following routine can be used as a guide to create a gentle home practice as well.

Begin in Savasana

Remain for a few minutes to create a steady, comfortable breath.

From supine (your back):

~ Leg pull: Bring right leg in to chest with knee bent for a leg pull. Other leg can be bent or remain straight if not uncomfortable. Hold five breaths.

~ Hip limbering: Circle the right knee to warm up the hip region for a few breaths.

~ Hamstring stretch: Extend the right leg up into a hamstring stretch. Hold five breaths.

~ Foot limbering: Breathing deeply, circle the right ankle, and then circle the whole right leg. Point the toes. Push through the ball of the foot and spread the toes. Flex the foot. Gently push the bottom of the foot inward. Gently push it outward. Circle the foot again.

~ Single leg lifts: From a hamstring stretch, inhale and lower the right leg halfway to the floor with the toes pointed. Exhale and flex the right foot to pull it back up. Repeat five to ten times. Go into:

~ Leg pull to adductor stretch: Inhale in right leg pull, exhale and take the bent knee outward to the side. Hold five breaths.

~ Leg pull to spinal twist: Inhale and pull right knee back to center. Exhale and guide bent knee over the straight leg on an exhalation. Go deeper, if comfortable, on your exhalations. Hold five to ten breaths.

~ Leg pull to tuck position: Pull the left knee in to meet up with the right.

~ Cradle rock: Cross at the ankles. Pull the knees gently apart with hands on shins. Gently rock side to side while breathing deeply for five to ten breaths.

Repeat entire supine sequence on the left side:

~ Take knees to side to come up slowly or rock right up to seated to:

~ Come to an all-fours position. Make sure knees are under hips and hands (with fingers and thumbs spread) are under shoulders. Place a blanket or towel under knees if it is uncomfortable. You may also come to a chair or to standing for alternative positions.

From all fours:

~ Cat/cow stretch: On an exhalation, round the back like an angry cat (draw chin to chest). This is cat stretch. On an inhalation, elongate the spine and look up (keeping the neck long). This is cow stretch. Repeat five to ten times.

~ Cat/cow/single leg: Add a single leg lift as you elongate the spine, by extending the right leg back on an inhalation. Look up. Then gently place the knee back down to the floor on an exhalation as you do the cat stretch. Take chin to chest. Repeat with left leg lifting on the inhale as you elongate the spine, knee back down for cat stretch on the exhalation. Repeat five to ten times, alternating sides. Add a Child's Pose in between each side, if you wish. Sink back into:

~ Child's Pose: Remain for five to ten breaths. Hands can go under forehead in the "two potato" position if your center of gravity is too high to comfortably place head to floor with arms stretched. Come back to all fours and take:

~ Thread the needle: Plan A—right elbow to the floor and left hand to hip. Twist gently to the left as you gaze to the left. Hold five breaths Plan B—thread the right arm through to come to shoulder and head. Minimal weight should be in the head. Use your core strength to keep spine long and effort distributed throughout the pose. Extend through the left arm and hold five breaths. Back to all fours to repeat by placing left elbow to the floor and twisting to the right (Plan A or B) for five breaths. Come back to all fours to place:

~ Right leg forward to lunge: *Skip this and remain in Child's Pose* if it bothers your back, knee, or hip region, or come gently to a standing or seated [in a chair] position to follow alternative positions, if necessary. Hands on hips or lift them overhead as you stretch into your hip flexors. Hold five to ten breaths before switching to left leg for five to ten breaths more. From all fours again, tuck toes under to come gently into:

~ Modified Downward Dog: Hold three to five breaths and then walk feet in to: Forward Bend

~ Forward Bend to (come slowly) to standing: Use hands pressing into thighs to come up with minimal pressure on the lower back.

From standing or seated in a chair:

The asanas below are all from the Standing Sequence section. (You may follow directions for these on pages 94–104.)

~ Triangle to Warrior II to side angle (right side): Hold each for three to five breaths then repeat left.

~ Tree Pose

Come gently from standing to seated:

The asanas below are all from the Primary Series section. (You may follow directions for these on pages 104–112.)

~ Forward Bend
~ Head to knee right, left
~ Straddle

Come gently from seated to reclining (supine):

The asanas below are all from the Closing Postures section. You may follow directions for these on pages 112–120.)

~Bridge
~Modified Shoulderstand
~Modified fish

Five to Ten Minutes in Savasana

The Gentle Routine suggested above can be done in approximately sixty minutes. It can be shortened by omitting asanas from various sections. Only have twenty minutes to practice? Take out the postures that are easy for you. Practice just those that you find challenging. This is one way to use the routine to create a more personalized program.

 **Going Deeper**

If you wish to learn more about Ashtanga vinyasa yoga, please visit the following websites:

http://www.ashtangayogacenter.com/
http://www.ashtanga.net/
http://www.ashtanga.com/
http://www.ionet.net/~tslade/yoga.htm
http://www.kpjayi.org/
http://www.rsharath.com/ashtanga.html
http://www.absolutelyashtanga.com/links.html

Highly recommended books on Ashtanga vinyasa yoga:

- Sri K. Pattabhi Jois. *Yoga Mala*. North Point Press, New York, New York 1999

- David Swenson. *Ashtanga Yoga: The Practice Manual: An Illustrated Guide to Personal Practice*. Ashtanga Yoga Productions, Austin, Texas,1999

- Gregor Maehle. *Ashtanga Yoga: Practice and Philosophy*. New World Library, Novato, CA 2006

- John Scott. *Ashtanga Yoga: The Definitive Step-by-Step Guide to Dynamic Yoga*. Gaia Books Limited London, 2000

Great Ashtanga vinyasa yoga DVDs:

- *Ashtanga Yoga: The Practice: The First Series*, by David Swenson

- *Ashtanga Yoga: The Practice: The Short Forms*, by David Swenson (both can be found at: http://www.ashtanga.net/)

- *Ashtanga Yoga Primary Series with Kino MacGregor* (www.ashtanga.com)

- *Ashtanga Yoga Primary Series with John Scott* (can be found at http://www.stillpointyoga.co.nz/ and at http://www.amazon.com)

- *Ashtanga Yoga Primary Series with Sharath Rangaswamy* (http://www.ashtangaproductions.com/)

- *Yoga With Richard Freeman: Ashtanga Yoga The Primary Series*

- *Yoga With Richard Freeman: Intro to Ashtanga Yoga* (both can be found on- http://www.yogaworkshop.com/)

Some things to know about Ashtanga yoga before going further:

1. **How to get started**

   Learn slowly and from a qualified teacher.

2. **Class particulars**

   For a morning practice, a very small amount of food can be taken to break your fast, but traditionally, it is recommended that no food is eaten for three hours prior to practice. It is also expected that you come well hydrated. Water bottles are not recommended in class. Towel off hands and feet *only* if the sweating becomes a danger.

Otherwise, continually wiping sweat becomes a distraction. Turn cell phones off, or better yet, leave them at home.

3. **Moon days**

   There "moon days" in Ashtanga yoga. In the Ashtanga tradition new and full moon days are observed as yoga holidays; one is not to practice on these days. All other days (with the exception of illness) are acceptable days to practice. The reasoning behind this has to do with the nature of Nature itself. We are energy beings. Just as the ocean tides are affected by moon days, so too are human beings. Because our physical composition is about 70% water, our energy is affected greatly by the moon's gravitational pull. When we learn to observe our body's natural rhythms, we can live in greater harmony with the Earth's rhythms.

4. **Mysore practice**

   Ashtanga vinyasa yoga comes from Mysore, India. That is why certain practices are called "Mysore." In the Ashtanga tradition, Mysore practice is a time to work on a series under the watchful eye of a teacher. It is a silent practice, with the exception of the invocation, breath, and the occasional assistance of an instructor.

5. **Contraindications**

   Menstrual cycle: It is generally recommended that women should not practice in the first few days of menses. However, many women report an improvement in period-related symptoms if they *do* practice; especially if they modify by doing a shorter, lighter practice. Premenstrual syndrome is improved dramatically for most women through a yoga practice. Inversions are generally not recommended during the menstrual cycle. Nature is trying to get rid of what is no longer needed with the help of gravity. Inversions interrupt this process. There continues to be debate on this subject. Listen to your body. A light practice with no inversions may be fine for you.

   Pregnancy: It is not advisable to begin an Ashtanga yoga practice while pregnant. A gentle, or prenatal, class would be more suitable. If however, you become pregnant after *years* of practice, asanas can be modified during your pregnancy.

Pranayama: The Control of Life Force

"Breath is central to yoga because it is central to life...and yoga is about Life."

—Yoga Master Krishnamacharya (1888–1989)

What Is Yogic Breathing?

All of us were born knowing how to breathe; we have been breathing all our lives. We average between 14,000 and 25,000 breaths daily. We usually take breathing for granted. We are typically not even conscious of every breath we take. Dr. Kathleen Hall (2006), founder of the Stress Institute, points out that "It is important to have reverent respect for our breath, it is the first thing we do as we come into the world, and the last experience we have when we leave."

Throughout our lives we have been given instructions on taking deep breaths when we are anxious or angry. According to the *Journal of Geriatric Society*, there is a physical benefit from this practice. Taking a few quiet breaths can actually cause blood pressure to drop and stay down for up to thirty minutes (Lasater, 2003).

We cannot deny the importance of breathing in our lives and also in our yoga practices. Breathing is at the heart of every posture practice, as well as our meditation. Through yoga, we stress the importance of observing each breath. When we begin to focus on our breath, we begin to focus on the present.

Scientists have shown that proper breathing can aid in pain control, elevate mood, relieve stress, and help ease a variety of other symptoms. In *The Psychology and Physiology of Breathing*, Dr. Robert Fried (1993) states that the medical profession has overlooked normal breathing. He finds in his studies that improper or shallow breathing could cause 50 to 70 percent of the medical complaints leading to some emotional and circulatory problems (Khalsa, 2000).

An ancient source for yoga practice is Patanjali's *Yoga Sutras*, which defines pranayama as mindful breathing. Pranayama is the fourth aspect of the eight limbs of yoga in the *Yoga Sutras*. In Sanskrit, the word *prana* means the life energy that fills the universe.

There are many reasons to breathe correctly: to discover how to breathe efficiently during yoga and meditation, to cope with stress, or to help control asthma or other respiratory illnesses. Proper breathing increases oxygen in the blood and in the brain.

Normal breathing is involuntary; it is automatic and effortless. Breathing on purpose, or voluntary breathing, should be deliberate and yet flowing. Yogic breathing is done through the nose by keeping the mouth closed. You should pause after each inhalation and exhalation. This may seem strange at first. If you feel the need to get more air, allow your breathing to return to automatic. It is important to breathe through the nose, if possible. The fine hairs in your nose act as a filter for germs and unwanted particles.

An easy way to get started is by focusing on your breath while practicing asana, or meditation, while walking or when commuting to work or school (Gates, 2000). Normal respiration begins with a slow and complete exhalation. The more complete the exhalation, the greater the quantity of fresh air to enter the lungs. Vital lung capacity is the total volume of air the lungs are able to contain.

Hatha yoga recognizes three separate forms of breathing: diaphragmatic, intercostal, and clavicular. Complete yogic breathing combines all three, which ultimately is the ideal technique. This is called Mahat Yoga Pranayama (Dykema, 2006), which means "great yoga breath." Another name for this breath is dirgha pranayama, which was explored further in the preceding chapter.

Diaphramatic Breathing

The diaphragm is a large, dome-shaped muscle that regulates respiration and is located directly below the lungs. During an inhalation, the diaphragm contracts and flattens. This creates an expansion of the chest cavity, which also pulls air into the lungs. The diaphragm moves back into position on the exhalation, forcing air from the lungs.

This technique is best practiced while lying down, relaxing the abdominal muscles. Exhale first, and then inhale. While the breath is drawn in, the abdomen expands. This fills the lower portion of the lungs.

Intercostal Breathing

The intercostals are the muscles between the ribs that aid the movement of the ribs required during respiration. Intercostal breathing is achieved by expanding the rib cage and chest wall through the inhalation. This fills the middle section of the lungs.

Clavicular Breathing

The clavicle is a bone on either side of your chest, which is commonly referred to as the collarbone. It connects your sternum (breastbone) to your shoulder. Clavicular breathing is created when air is inhaled, raising the shoulders and collarbone, filling the upper portion of the lungs.

Complete Breathing (Three-Part Breathing)

This breath begins in the diaphragm, expanding the abdomen, rib cage, chest, shoulders and clavicles with each inhalation.

*Beginners should try to practice five to ten minutes each day, starting with diaphragmatic breathing. As practice continues, the student may work up to complete yogic breathing, or three-part breathing. When practicing, always be aware of proper alignment and posture whether sitting or lying down.

 ## Organs Used in Breathing

Nose and Mouth

We breathe through the nose, primarily to warm and filter air before it enters the lungs. In terms of yogic philosophy, breathing through the nose also stimulates the central nervous system.

Larynx and Pharynx

The larynx, also known as the "voice box," controls the muscles that produce sound. At the top of the larynx is the epiglottis, which closes tightly to prevent food or liquid from passing through. The pharynx is the opening behind the nose and part of the respiratory system, which ends at the esophagus. It is part of the digestive system as well.

Trachea and Bronchi

The trachea, also known as the windpipe, is the passage that moves air from the larynx to the bronchi. The end of the trachea is split into two bronchi with branches called bronchioles, leading to alveoli where gas exchange happens.

Lungs and Thorax

The lungs are the main organs responsible for respiration in the thoracic region. The lungs function is to transfer oxygen into the bloodstream. The thoracic cavity contains the heart and lungs.

When Should You Use Yogic Breathing?

Of course, yogic breathing is especially helpful during asana practice. A general rule when practicing asana is to inhale as your body extends and exhale as your body folds, or goes deeper in the pose. Throughout the day yogic breathing can be incredibly beneficial. Practicing before bed can help relax the mind and body. Taking a few deep breaths before studying, taking a test, or prior to an important meeting or performance, can calm the nervous system and clear the mind. Research has found that anytime you are in a stressful situation, mindful breathing can help to restore calmness.

Adapted from pages 91–94, 95–100 of *Yoga for Students* by Nicole Magnan Caruso, Kirstin Brekken Shea, Dottiedee Agnor, Beth Netherland, Kristin Slagel and Teri Wenzel. Copyright © 2007. Reprinted by permission of Kendall Hunt Publishing Company.

Below are some pranayama ratios recommended by instructor John Calabria for a variety of situations:

For an increase in energy:

	Inhale		Retention		Exhale		Retention
	6	:	4	:	6	:	1

For balance:

	Inhale		Retention		Exhale		Retention
	6	:	2	:	6	:	2
or	8	:	1	:	8	:	1

For relaxation:

	Inhale		Retention		Exhale		Retention
	6	:	1	:	8	:	4
or	6	:	1	:	10	:	1
or	4	:	1	:	12	:	1
or	4	:	1	:	8	:	4

You should look for a highly trained Yoga teacher with vast knowledge in pranayama to offer you the guidance and supervision required for more advanced methods of breath control.

9

Meditation

"Meditation is simply about being yourself and knowing about who that is. It is about coming to realize that you are on a path whether you like it or not, namely the path that is your life."

—Jon Kabat-Zinn

"Only that day dawns to which we are awake."

—Henry David Thoreau

 ## What Is Meditation?

The seventh limb of yoga's eight-limbed path is dhyana, or meditation. The *Yoga Sutras* refers to it as a steady, continuous flow of attention directed to the same point or region. Webster defines *meditate* as to plan or intend, to think deeply, ponder, study or reflect. Meditation is also referred to as the relaxation response. Dr. Herbert Benson of Harvard created this term in his studies on stress in 1967. He discovered through his research that individuals who practiced meditation, significantly lowered their blood pressure, heart rates, and increased their theta brain waves causing higher norepinephrine levels (Hall 2006). An imbalance of norepinephrine and serotonin plays a role in depression and pain. Meditation has been proven to help balance these chemicals. Balance is the key.

Meditation helps us to become more "mindful". It helps us to pay attention, quiet the mind, and reach "present moment awareness," which involves listening to your heart. These things lead us to peace of mind, serenity, and an appreciation for the moment through a journey of self-discovery. Learning to live in the moment may sound easy, but it takes patience.

Cesare Pavese once said, "We do not remember days; we remember moments." Martha Graham put it this way when speaking of dance: "All that is important is this one moment in movement. Make the moment vital and worth living. Do not let it slip away unnoticed and unused"(Kabat-Zinn 1994).

We usually take these qualities for granted. We come to realize the importance of "mindfulness" through meditation practice. Only then can we begin to be fully present on the path that we are traveling.

According to Dr. Jon Kabat-Zinn (1994), creator of the MBSR (Mindfulness Based Stress Reduction) technique, and founder of the Stress Reduction Clinic and the Center for Mindfulness in Medicine, Health Care, and Society,

"Mindfulness provides a simple but powerful route for getting ourselves unstuck, back in touch with our wisdom and vitality; taking charge of the direction and quality of our lives, including relationships with our family, work, with the world, and fundamentally, our relationship with our self as a person."

Benefits of Meditation

One of the biggest and most underestimated health issues that we face as a society is stress. Stress contributes to a variety of health problems regardless of age. We have conditioned ourselves to be multitaskers. We try to juggle so many things at once that we don't even realize that we risking our health. School, work, family, friends, relationships, meetings…you name it; we try to cram everything into our day. Many use expensive gadgets to remind them when and where to go, utilizing every waking hour of the day for something "productive." Many people go through a crammed day with headphones on, never realizing the chaos that is being created. The result of this inner and outer overload is undeniable: a whole host of disorders related to stress that can eventually lead to a number of diseases.

Ultimately we all seek the opposite of stress. Dr. Kathleen Hall (2006), founder of the Stress Institute states, "Peace of mind, body, and soul is what we all want to experience. Serenity is the opposite of stress." A regular meditation practice can help us dramatically in our quest for serenity.

Over ten million American adults say they practice some form of meditation. Meditation practice is being recommended by physicians and other members of the medical community to help alleviate some of the physical, psychological, and emotional problems resulting from chronic stress.

Research has proven that meditation can:

- Lower blood pressure
- Improve sleep patterns
- Improve symptoms of chronic pain
- Lower cholesterol
- Improve the immune system
- Help prevent heart disease
- Help prevent strokes
- Ease symptoms of premenstrual syndrome (PMS)
- Improve irritable bowel syndrome (IBS)
- Decrease pain from fibromyalgia
- Increase IQ
- Enhance creativity
- Improve perceptual and short term memory testing
- Improve moral reasoning

Meditation has been found to be extremely helpful to individuals who are undergoing cancer treatment or experiencing other forms of chronic illness. Dr. Ainslie Meares, an Australian psychiatrist, is one of the many physicians who now uses meditation with cancer patients. He has found his patients report significant reductions in anxiety, as well as less discomfort and pain, thus improving their quality of life.

The physical benefits of meditation are overwhelming and undisputable, but the spiritual, mental, and psychological benefits are the reasons most choose to practice meditation.

At the University of Wisconsin, Dr. Richard Davidson found that meditation improves the immune system. A study reported in *The Journal of Memory and Cognition* found that college students who meditate had significant improvements on perceptual and short-term memory tests. Other studies have proven an increase in brain wave coherence associated with an increase in creativity, improved moral reasoning, and higher IQ through meditation.

A study published in the *Alcoholism Treatment Quarterly* and the *International Journal of Addictions* reports that meditation can also decrease cigarette, alcohol, and drug abuse (Hall 2006).

Psychological benefits of meditation include a decrease in:

- Anxiety

- Depression

- Irritability

- Moodiness

And an increase in:

- Feelings of happiness

- Feelings of vitality

- Emotional stability

- Spirituality

 **How to Meditate**

Meditation is not about feeling a certain way. It is about feeling the way you feel.
—Osho International Foundation, *Meditation: The First and Last Freedom*

The important thing to remember is *keep it simple*. Mindfulness is moment to moment observation. With compassion and patience, this pure awareness creates the ability to awaken to the beauty of each moment. We tend to complicate these moments with over-thinking. Don't begin meditation practice and think, "Okay, now what?" or "Am I doing this right?" In our fast-paced world, it will take some time to learn to slow down the mind. In *Wherever You Go, There You Are*, Dr. Jon Kabat-Zinn (1994) states, "It is sufficient to make a little time in your life for stillness and what we call non-doing, and then tune into your breathing." A common mistake people make when beginning a meditation practice is trying to force the brain to shut off or manipulate the mind to solve all of your problems. But calming the mind will help you learn to deal with the issues on your life through a more peaceful means.

If thoughts creep in, deal with those thoughts and move on. Too many individuals make the mistake of trying to force thoughts out of the mind, causing tension. Just relax and let your mind be. Kabat-Zinn (1994) quotes a poster from the seventies of a yogi riding the Hawaiian waves. The caption reads: "You can't stop the waves, but you can learn to surf". Thoughts will keep coming. You can let the waves take over and fight the thoughts, or you can learn to relax and ride them through your mind.

You may begin by practicing five to ten minutes, working up to twenty or thirty. As stated earlier, even five minutes of mindful meditation can be helpful.

Some Helpful Tips for Meditation

- Find a quiet place with few distractions.

- Try to use the same place and time each day.

- Sit with knees below naval and spine elongated. Place your hands gently in your lap. This can be done:

in a chair with feet hip width apart and flat on the floor

on a cushion or block on the floor

or in a specific meditation position such as:

Easy pose

Cobblers pose

Yoga pose photos in this chapter courtesy of Rachel Donley.

144

or on a meditation bench

In half lotus or in full lotus

- Close your eyes or gaze softly at an object that is calming.

- Repeat an affirmation or a mantra, if you wish, to settle and soothe the mind. This can be a word or short phrase.

- Observe your breath. Feel it from the moment it enters your nostrils to the moment it is released.

- Watch thoughts come and go without attachment; each time return to the breath and/or to the word or phrase of choice.

When to Meditate

Choosing when to meditate depends on each individual and, of course, his or her lifestyle. Some like to practice meditation in the morning before the day begins. This takes a commitment to choose to awaken early and start your day in a calm, peaceful manner. The way you start your typically dictates how the rest of your day evolves. For example, if you sleep through your alarm and you are rushed to begin your day, the rest of the day seems rushed and chaotic. If you begin your day in a tranquil manner, your day usually goes a lot smoother.

Anytime that you can use some "quiet time" will beneficial. What is important is that you create the time in your day and it becomes a routine part of your day that you always schedule around.

Walking meditation is a very popular and effective means to practice. A walk in the woods, by a lake, or even in your neighborhood park can help relax the mind and improve physical fitness.

"Breathwalk" is the science of combining specific patterns of breathing synchronized with the art of directed, meditative attention (Khalsa 2000). This type of walking meditation has been used not only to rejuvenate the body, mind, and spirit but also is used to treat certain physical, mental, and emotional illnesses.

The meditation practice is a journey of growth and development. It helps us to explore ourselves and find peace of mind. "Perhaps the most spiritual thing any of us can do is simply to look through our own eyes, see with eyes of wholeness, and act with integrity and kindness" (Kabat-Zinn 1994).

Having a mind that is at peace with itself, a mind that is clear and joyous is the basis of happiness and compassion.

—Susan Piver

What lies behind us and what lies before us are tiny matters compared to what lies within us.

—Ralph Waldo Emerson

Test Your Knowledge

Name _____ **Date** _____

1. List ten physical and/or psychological benefits of meditation.

   1.

   2.

   3.

   4.

   5.

   6.

   7.

   8.

   9.

   10.

2. List three positions recommended for meditation.

3. List three tips for meditation that you feel would be particularly helpful.

For a Full Week:

Make a commitment to yourself to awaken five minutes earlier in order to sit and mediate for five full minutes. Journal your experiences, and if it was helpful at the end of the first week, add another week and another five minutes. In time you will break your old cycle of "automatic pilot," and begin your day with some clarity.

For One Day this Week

Throughout the day, practice the following affirmation, taken from the book, *Peace Is Every Step*, by Thich Nhat Hanh (1991):

- On inhalation: "Breathing in, I calm my mind."

- On exhalation: "Breathing out, I smile."

Now abbreviate this to:

- (On inhalation): Calm

- (On exhalation): Smile

How did it impact your day? Journal your experience, if you wish. If it was a positive experience, do it again tomorrow! And the next day, and the next day…

Suggested Readings

Osho International Foundation. 1999. *Meditation: The First and Last Freedom.*

Jon Kabat-Zinn. 1994. *Wherever You Go, There You Are: Mindfulness Meditation in Everyday Life,* Hyperion.

Thich Nhat Hanh. 1991. *Peace Is Every Step: The Path of Mindfulness in Everyday Life.*

You, the Yogic Consumer

 ## You Are What You Eat

How often have you heard that statement without giving it a nanosecond of thought? Yet—to the extent that what we put in our mouths, chew, swallow and digest is absorbed to eventually be transported to the very cells that make up our body—we truly are what we eat. The statistics on overweight, obesity, and weight-related diseases in the United States are both disturbing and shocking.

In "Prevalence and Trends in Obesity Among U.S. Adults, 1999–2008," an abstract published in *The Journal of the American Medical Association* (January 2010), clinicians Katherine M. Flegal, Ph.D., Margaret D. Carroll, MSPH, Cynthia L. Ogden, Ph.D., and Lester R. Curtain, Ph.D., concluded that the prevalence of obesity in the United States exceeds 30 percent for adults over twenty years of age. These statistics don't even include the numbers of people who are overweight.

During a lecture at West Chester University a few years ago, Dr. Mehmet Oz commented about the state of our collective health in America when he said "We are mortgaging our future," not only personally, but as a country, with the food choices we are making.

The human tongue is designed to experience a variety of tastes, yet the standard **A**merican **d**iet (SAD) is such that we really experience only a few: Think of a typical fast-food meal….

According to Eric Schlosser (2002) in *Fast Food Nation: The Dark Side of the All-American Meal*, Americans now spend over $110 billion on fast food each year. In addition, every day about one-quarter of the U.S. population eats fast food. This statistic would not have to be so scary if the "fast" food we were consuming in such quantities would be fresh food. Why isn't it? It *is* available. The sad truth is that we are demanding fast food to sustain the incredibly unhealthy lifestyles *we* are creating. So why would most companies want to change something that is not (financially) broken?

Most companies' bottom lines are not concerned with the size of *our* bottoms or even the state of our health, but rather with the profitability of the company. They are just providing us with what we are demanding, but what if we started asking for better, fresher, more healthful food? Would they listen? Interestingly, some already are.

Another surprising statistic is the amount of money Americans spend each year on the diet industry. While figures vary among a number of reporting agencies, a safe estimate would be forty-five billion dollars…yes, *billion*. Numerous reports indicate that 90 to 95 percent of all Americans who have spent money on the diet industry (for weight loss) end up gaining the weight back within the year. The ridiculous part of all of this is that we likely learned how to gain, lose, or maintain weight from basic math concepts learned in elementary school.

For example:

- Calories Eaten > Calories Burned = Weight Gain
- Calories Eaten < Calories Burned = Weight Loss
- Calories Eaten = Calories Burned = No Change

Nutrition 101

Considering the Earth's bounty and our myriad food choices, it seems a shame that the word *diet* often is interpreted as a four-letter word; a "bad" word that implies restriction. The basic components of a healthy diet (all the things that nourish us) include the proper amount of the following nutrients, according to age, height, weight, and activity level:

- Protein (found in nuts, nut butters, beans and other legumes, fish, meat, poultry, dairy products, and eggs)
- Fat (found in animal and dairy products, nuts, and oils)
- Carbohydrates (found in fruits, vegetables, pasta, rice, grains, beans, legumes, sugars, starches, and fibers)
- Vitamins (such as vitamins A, B, C, D, E, and K)
- Minerals (such as calcium, potassium, and iron)
- Water

Not all sources of these essential nutrients are equal in terms of our health and well-being. Knowing what to eat and how much to eat can seem a bit overwhelming, but empowering yourself with knowledge is the best way to tackle this topic with confidence. The websites below offer some fantastic information on nutrition:

http://www.mayoclinic.com/health/vegetarian-diet/hq01596
http://www.cspinet.org
http://www.ewg.org/foodscores

The Three Gunas

According to yogic philosophy, there are three qualities of energy that exist in all things in the universe. The Sanskrit word for these qualities is *guna*. Knowing even a little bit about these qualities can be useful in our quest to create balance in our lives.

The three gunas are:

Sattva: Calm, centered, compassionate, pure, fresh, light.
Rajas: Changing, stimulating, passionate, frenetic, spicy, acidic, sour. Eating (or doing anything) in a hurry is rajasic.
Tamas: Inertia, dull, sluggish, dark, heavy, stale, fermented, over- or underripe. Overeating or overdoing anything is tamasic.

Right at this very moment in space, there are stars that are new, stars that are changing, and stars that are burning out, or dying off. Meanwhile, inside your body there are cells that possess all these same qualities. Food is energy and part of nature—therefore having the same properties.

If you have a prior knowledge of basic nutrition, choosing and eating food according to the gunas actually simplifies nourishment dramatically.

Imagine taking a bite of a perfectly ripe organic apple, just plucked from the tree. That apple would give your body the most sattvic energy that apple could possibly give. Now imagine that you put that apple in your coat pocket, only to discover it there a week later. Now that apple is rajasic. It is changing. There are likely spots and bruises on it by now. Eating the apple in this state would provide your body with proportionate energy. Let's envision that same apple months later, pulled from your refrigerator. It is wrinkled and shriveled, so you crush it up, add some ingredients, and let it become vinegar or wine. That once beautiful, nutritious apple now possesses the lowest quality of energy. It is tamasic.

Eating to Support Your Health and Your Yoga Practice

In terms of eating well, we would be wise to choose pure, fresh foods and limit consumption of foods that offer our bodies and minds a lower quality of energy. As far as your yoga practice goes, you will be able to notice the difference in how calm, steady, and energized you will feel on the days you have nourished your body well. Through observation of the way food choices affect practice, you will be motivated to continue to make the kinds of choices that allow you to care for yourself on all levels.

Food is everywhere. Besides the obvious places, like the grocery store and restaurants, we now find tempting snacks almost anywhere we go and at almost any *time* we may be out and about. Fast-food chains set up shop in gas stations. Groceries and junk food can now be found in drugstores and "big box" stores. Vending machines abound and are filled with some of the most tamasic food available.

In *Nutrition Action Healthletter* (May 2010), which addresses how the food industry drives us to overeat, Yale University Professor Kelly Brownell says, "It's difficult to avoid obesity in a toxic food environment. There's a tremendous pressure on people to overeat." It is not surprising that two out of every three adults and one of every three children in the United States are overweight or obese.

Have you ever noticed at fine restaurants that the food quality is higher but the quantity is reduced? While most people don't have the extra money to frequent these restaurants, perhaps we would all be wiser to consider skipping the numerous trips to fast-food places in order to save up for an occasional healthful meal served by folks who truly appreciate food and the well-being of the people who eat it.

Several fast-food chains are known for serving up large plates of food that people may not only justify ordering but also consider a value, knowing they will take part of it home to eat another time. Here's the problem: You will eat more of what wasn't good for you in the first place—just at a different time.

Thankfully, we are becoming wiser about the food industry with the popularity of books and videos on the subject, many of which are listed within and at the end of this chapter.

Some basic things to consider that may help you be a wiser (and healthier) consumer:

- Every dollar you spend is a *vote* you are casting. Do you want to vote for a large corporation that places profit before people? Or do you want to vote *"yes!"* for your health and the health of the planet?

- The further food gets away from its original intention (the whole food), the further it goes toward a lower quality of energy. Is food in a box with loads of ingredients (some of which you may not even recognize) even *really* food?

- The grocery store is set up to offer fresher foods around its perimeter. Thankfully, most grocery chains now have an organic section.

- How fresh can certain foods really be if they are traveling thousands of miles to get to your store?

- What is the environmental impact of the food you are purchasing? Does it use vast amounts of land and resources to produce? Are chemical fertilizers, herbicides, and pesticides used to produce this food?

- Are there unreasonable amounts of resources used in the packaging of the food items (or any items) you are purchasing?

- What are the social and spiritual implications of the food? Do living beings (humans or animals) suffer in order to provide you with nourishment and enjoyment from this food?

Eating in tune with yogic principles, you would consider all of the above. The same thoughtfulness used to purchase or harvest your own food would go into the preparation and enjoyment of the food. Preparing and serving food with love, care, and attention, as well as eating mindfully, are all part of eating like a yogin.

A Yogic Diet: The Vegetarian Question

Vegetarianism

Most yoga practitioners choose not to eat meat as an act of reverence for all of life. It is a personal decision. Those who choose vegetarianism usually do so with ahimsa, or nonviolence, in mind. Some vegetarians still choose to eat eggs and dairy products, as an animal does not *need* to be harmed for one to be nourished from these items.

There are many categories of vegetarianism, many which constitute a flexitarian, or semi-vegetarianism diet. These newer categories make more sense to most people, since no matter how you look at vegetarianism, something that had a face was *never* a vegetable. For example, a "pesco vegetarian" chooses to eat fish, seafood, and dairy. The health benefits from consuming *certain* fish are undeniable. A vegan, or an individual who consumes nothing that comes from an animal, would choose to replace nutrients found in animal products with foods offering equivalent nutrition, such as soy milk fortified with vitamin B-12, one of the micronutrients difficult to get in a vegan diet. For a vegan, perfect proteins (with all the essential amino acids) are found in certain grains, as well as in bean and grain combinations.

The greatest challenge for any of us, regardless of our personal choice, is to be tolerant and to make an effort to be as nonjudgmental as possible. A student once joked, "Don't you hear those vegetables screaming when you cut them?" There are indeed ways to justify any decision you might make. The important thing is that you approach your personal decision equipped with information.

Most yoga practitioners begin to eventually phase out foods considered to be rajasic or tamasic and eat the most sattvic diet possible. Many yogins choose vegetarianism for this purpose, as well as for animal welfare issues. Mahatma Gandhi once said that "The greatness of a society and its moral progress can be judged by the way it treats its animals."

According to *The Sivananda Companion to Yoga* (2000), the following foods are:

Sattvic:

Whole-grain cereals and breads	Legumes
Fresh fruits and vegetables	Nuts, seeds, and sprouted seeds
Pure fruit juices	Honey
Milk, butter, and cheese	Herb teas

Obviously, choosing these items locally and/or organically grown or produced would help to ensure that you are getting food that would be the most sattvic, thus leading to a calm, "peaceful mind in control of a fit body" (Yoga Vedanta Center 2000).

Rajasic:

- Very bitter, hot, sour, dry, or salty foods
- Sharp spices and strong herbs
- Stimulants such as eggs, coffee, tea, and chocolate

Such foods, consumed in moderation, may be acceptable—especially to help create more balance if you were "stuck" in a dark or dull (tamasic) energy state.

Tamasic:

- Meat
- Fermented foods such as alcohol and vinegar
- Tobacco
- Stale or overripe foods

A serious yogin would avoid consuming any of these products.

A Yogic Approach to Consumerism

Below is a list of some of the many things to reflect on regarding eating and shopping in tune with yogic principles.

If Possible, Grow Your Own Food

This requires a lot less space than you may think. If you have an outside space that gets at least four hours of sunlight, you may be able to create a simple container garden. Consider using an organic growing medium rather than one that is laced with chemicals. Growing your own fresh herbs, lettuces, and cherry tomatoes can be mastered without much room, and the difference in taste and nutritional value is remarkable.

Buy Fresh and Buy Local. Buy Organic When Possible

Most communities offer farmers markets throughout the week during the growing season. Find out where you can go to purchase fresh food. You may even find many markets within a few miles of where you live. These farmers markets are often spread throughout the week, allowing you to eat fresh all week long. Look for vendors who may be offering organically grown fruits and vegetables, or at least pesticide- and herbicide-free produce. Some markets may even offer meat, eggs, and dairy products. By eating fresher, more sattvic foods, you will not only be fueling yourself with more nutritious food, but you will also be helping your local farmer.

StockPhotosLV/Shutterstock.com

natalia bulatova/
Shutterstock.com

Olha Afanasieva/Shutterstock.com

Additionally, most communities have CSAs, or community-supported agriculture. Basically, a local farmer offers a certain number of "shares" (boxes of produce and other items from that farm), and when a consumer purchases a membership to that particular CSA, he or she then receives a weekly share throughout the growing season.

The websites below can help you to locate fresh food, learn more about the importance of eating fresh, and support the local economy:

www.foodroutes.org

www.buylocalpa.org

www.localharvest.org

www.eatwellguide.org

http://www.youtube.com/watch?v=IOYhM2c8PmM

http://www.sustainabletable.org/home.php

http://www.greenamericatoday.org/

Know Where Your Food Comes From

Most people want to know where their food comes from. Thankfully, this is now much easier with the creation of the United States Department of Agriculture (USDA) Country of Origin Labeling (COOL) legislation that is now law (**http://www.ams.usda.gov/AMSv1.0/cool**).

If you are a meat eater, or you eat eggs, poultry, fish, or shellfish, learn more about those industries. If possible, find local farms to purchase these products to get the highest quality of energy from them. If you enjoy eating fish (fresh or saltwater) or shellfish, learn more about sustainable fishing and which fish we should be avoiding (**http://www.edf.org/page.cfm?tagID=1521**).

As a society, we are, for the most part, anesthetized to the horrors of the meat industry. Meat eaters can go to the grocery store and purchase most of these products on white, or pastel-colored trays without having to give much thought to the conditions that preceded the slaughter or even the conditions at the time of slaughter. In some countries, you might find the head of the animal beside the meat of that animal at the meat counter of the grocery store. While this may seem disturbing, at least there is some thought given to the fact that that animal was slaughtered to provide sustenance. In this way, there is some reverence for the animal.

The following terms will hopefully help you understand the meat, dairy, and poultry industries a little better:

Cage-free: Purchasing eggs labeled cage-free assures that these animals can lay their eggs in nests, walk, and spread their wings. According to the Humane Society of the United States, these are "tangible benefits that shouldn't be underestimated." Cage-free may not be cruelty-free, however, as many of these animals have their beaks altered in what is likely an incredibly painful procedure (**http://www.humanesociety.org**).

Grass-fed: Grass-fed animals eat a diet that is natural to them; they graze outside and are not sent to feed lots to be fattened. As a result, the use of antibiotics often is unnecessary. There is an art and science to this method, and the result is apparently tender, more nutritious meat and fewer environmental implications (**http://www.eatwild.com/basics.html**). The standards set by the USDA in October 2007 have helped to curb the degradation of the term *grass-fed* by unscrupulous ranchers wishing to be a part of the new "food revolution."

Natural: Your best bet as a consumer is to avoid the descriptions on the front of the package and look at the ingredient list on the side. "All natural" or "natural" claims are placed on the front of packaged food items by the manufacturer and really don't amount to much. Foods can be structurally or chemically altered and still be considered all natural, because this is not yet regulated by the FDA. A good example is corn. Whole-grain corn is healthful. We now know, however, that high-fructose corn (altered corn) syrup contributes significantly to overweight, obesity, and diseases related to those conditions.

Organic: J.I. and Robert Rodale, pioneers in organic farming, knew long ago that soil conditions and the way in which food is grown would have a dramatic impact on nutrition and food quality. Healthy food comes from healthy soil (**http://rodaleinstitute.org**), which means soil that has not been altered synthetically with chemical herbicides, pesticides, and fertilizers.

According to the USDA, organic production is a system that is managed in accordance with the Organic Foods Production Act of 1990 (OFPA). In order to carry the "USDA Organic" label, farmers must adhere to the rules and regulations (**http://www.ams.usda.gov/AMSv1.0/nop**). If you are paying more for organic items that are not labeled USDA Organic, you are taking a bit of a financial risk, as the standards need to be uniformly higher to ensure that consumers are indeed getting foods for which they are paying extra.

Free range: In a perfect world this would mean that the animals were able to forage outside to consume a diet that was natural and intended for that animal. Currently, it basically means that the animal may spend some time outdoors. If it could just…get…to…that door leading outside.

Hormone-free: This term is self-explanatory. If a company has taken the time to label the product as such, it is likely truly free of added synthetic hormones, most of which are to accelerate growth or keep a dairy cow lactating.

Learn More about the Companies You Are Supporting

It can be surprising to discover that some of the companies you may be "voting" for may not support your own personal values. Conversely, in some cases, you will discover companies doing innovative and inspiring things. Investigate.

Know How to Be Safety-Minded When Choosing and Eating Foods

Organic produce typically costs more than conventionally grown (with chemicals) produce. However, we would be smart to purchase as many organic foods as possible for our own health and the health of the planet. The more we demand it, the sooner the changes will come.

In August 2009, *Good Morning America* aired a story about the safety of produce in the United States. According to thousands of government tests done on produce, most fruits and vegetables had only trace amounts of pesticide residue. Based on research by The Environmental Working Group (2009), however, twelve fruits and vegetables are known as **"The Dirty Dozen"**(www.ewg.org):

Peaches	Strawberries
Apples	Kale
Bell peppers	Lettuce
Celery	Imported grapes
Cherries	Pears
Nectarines	Carrots

To limit pesticide exposure, consider purchasing the fruits and vegetable listed above from sources that have grown the produce organically. Before eating any produce, wash it under running water, and use a vegetable brush on produce to remove pesticide residue and potentially harmful bacteria.

The Center for Science in the Public Interest (CSPI), a consumer advocacy group funded solely by individuals and private foundation grants, has done much to create positive change in the food industry Due to the increased incidence of food-borne illnesses, such as the *E. coli* and *Salmonella* outbreaks in recent years, the group compiled their own "Dirty Dozen," which was expounded in the December 2006 issue of *Nutrition Action*. The cover story, "Fear of Fresh," tackles food-borne illness caused by harmful bacteria that may end up in fresh produce, meats, dairy, nuts, sprouts, shellfish, and fish (www.cspinet.org).

Create Time to Purchase and Prepare Your Own "Fast Food"

Keep containers (preferably glass ones with lids) filled with "grab and go" cut vegetables, prepared snacks, salads, etc., in your refrigerator. Buy organic apples and bananas (if you do not have allergies to those things) every week and eat one *every*day. Look for biodegradable sandwich baggies (brown waxed-paper bags are great) or a reusable stainless steel container to tote healthful snacks or sandwiches during the day. Make your own trail mix. and keep it in a large (preferably glass) container so that you can easily scoop out a portion.

Limit Salt Intake

There is a great deal of sodium in most processed and manufactured foods. Too much salt in our daily diet can contribute to hypertension, stroke, and heart disease. Salt elevates blood pressure, so people with high blood pressure need to be extra careful to avoid getting too much. The Centers for Disease Control and Prevention's (CDC) *Morbidity and Mortality Weekly Report* (March 27, 2009) states that Americans are consuming more than twice the healthy amount—most of which is coming from processed foods.

This is not an issue if your diet consists of mostly fresh, not processed, foods.

Avoid Products with High-Fructose Corn Syrup and Added Sugar

High-fructose corn syrup (HFCS) is a sweetener and preservative made from highly processed corn. It has been used in the United States since the 1950s as a cheap alternative to sweeten foods and medicines. It is difficult to find foods, beverages, or even cough syrup products that do *not* contain HFCS. Numerous studies have been done to determine if and how HFCS

affects metabolism, weight gain, and health in general. Recent research at Princeton University, reported in March 2010, indicates that HFCS actually causes weight gain (**http://www.princeton. edu/main/news/archive/S26/91/22K07/**). So much of our food has added sugars that our body does not even need. We can no longer ignore the science that shows how addictive and damaging sugar is for human health. Obesity, tooth decay, and numerous life-threatening diseases are now linked to consuming too much sugar. Public Health advocates and Scientists scored a huge victory in 2015 when the FDA endorsed a proposed revision to the current "Nutrition Facts" label that will show the amount of added sugar in a product. Find more information here: http://www.hsph .harvard.edu/nutritionsource/carbohydrates/added-sugar-in-the-diet/.

Learn how to find and consume high-quality protein. The amount of protein we need to consume on a daily basis is determined by age, activity level, and special needs, such as pregnancy. Protein quality is dependent on the nutritional amounts of amino acids, which are needed for overall health. Animal proteins such as eggs, milk, cheese, meat, and fish are considered high-quality (complete) protein sources; however, the yogic perspective would also consider the conditions under which this protein was produced. For example, could we really regard the protein we are getting from an animal treated inhumanely as "high quality"? Plant proteins—such as those from nuts, grains, corn, seeds, legumes, beans, fruits, and vegetable—lack a proper balance of amino acids and are therefore referred to as incomplete proteins. Combining incomplete proteins (such as beans and rice) within a single meal or even within a few hours can deliver the correct balance of all essential amino acids and is not as difficult as many perceive. Quinoa is an amazing source for complete protein that has been grown and eaten for five thousand years. Although not completely accurate, quinoa is considered to be a grain. Quinoa is a wonderful ingredient that can be used in countless recipes to provide superior nutrition.

Eat More Complex Carbohydrates to Get Plenty of Fiber

Complex carbohydrates provide us with slow, sustained energy and are found in such foods as fruits, legumes, starchy vegetables, nuts, seeds, grains, whole-grain breads, and whole-grain cereals. Whole grains contain significant dietary fiber, which is important for a number of reasons. According to the Mayo Clinic, dietary fiber not only aids waste elimination but also helps to control blood sugar and to lower blood cholesterol (**http://www.mayoclinic.com/health/fiber/nu00033**).

In addition to eating more of the items mentioned above, you can increase dietary fiber by adding things such as ground flax, wheat germ, or even dried or fibrous fresh fruits to cereals, yogurt, soups, etc.

Eat Real Food

Real food has no food label. You can't get much easier than that!

Learn More about Genetically Modified Organisms (GMOs)

A quick online search for information on this topic will yield an enormous amount of information, some of which will be enlightening, some of which will be disturbing. Considering the controversial nature of this topic, we would all be wise to inform ourselves.

Purchase a Stainless Steel Water Bottle, or Recycle a Glass Bottle to Reuse—Advocate for Alternatives at Stores and Restaurants

Consider filtering your tap water. Most tap water in the United States is of an acceptable quality. A good filtering system is a much more economically and environmentally sustainable way to have access to high-quality water through the day. If you have municipal water, check the quality. You can find information regarding the quality of your community's water online. If you have a well, have your water analyzed every year or so to be sure of its quality before using it to filter.

As reported in the June 2007 *Consumer Reports* online issue of *Greener Choices*, the National Resources Defense Council (NRDC) concluded after a four-year study, that there is no assurance that bottled water is any safer than tap water. In fact, laboratory tests have shown that as much as 25 percent of all bottled water sold in the United States is essentially tap water. Fossil fuels are used in the packaging and transportation of bottled water, leading to sizable energy costs. The plastic most commonly used to make water bottles is polyethylene terephthalate (PET #1). It is made from crude oil. Americans' demand for bottled water requires more than 1.5 million barrels of oil annually, which is enough to fuel about one hundred thousand cars every year, according to the Earth Policy Institute. Unfortunately, billions of these bottles end up in landfills every year due to the low recycling rate of water bottles in general. "According to Dr. Gina Solomon, senior scientist at the NRDC, about 4,000 tons of carbon dioxide (CO_2)—a major greenhouse gas— are emitted during the transportation of bottled water from France, Italy, and Fiji to the U.S." (Greenerchoices.org, 2007).

Make filling your water bottle a part of your morning routine, and refilling it throughout the day, a priority. Try to drink more water and limit sodas and other beverages.

Consider Purchasing a Few Good Cloth Bags for Shopping—Advocate for Plastic Bag Alternatives at Stores and Restaurants

The use of plastic bags continues to devastate the environment. Most plastic bags—produced quite inexpensively in other countries—are created from crude oil and natural gas: fossil fuels.

According to the Worldwatch Institute, Americans throw out over one hundred billion plastic bags each year, yet not even 1 percent of those are recycled. The good news is that in 2007 San Francisco banned plastic bags, which seems to have sparked an interest among environmental groups and many politicians. (http://www.worldwatch.org/node/1499). Many grocery chains are voluntarily cutting back on the use of plastic bags, and some stores are now using biodegradable bags made from corn or spent sugar cane. Biodegradable bags, utensils, as well as unbleached napkins are available at some restaurants now as well.

Consider Sustainable Fibers

Numerous sustainable options for clothing and other material goods exist today. When purchasing clothing or goods made from fibers, you should remember to check the tags to determine the material content.

A white T-shirt made from conventionally grown cotton goes through dozens of processes before ending up in the store. Globally, conventional cotton producers use almost 2.6 billion dollars' worth of pesticides each year, which accounts for more than 10 percent of the world's annual pesticide use and almost 25 percent of the insecticides used annually (http://www.panna.org/resources/cotton). Because cotton is difficult to grow without the use of large quantities of chemicals (pesticides, fertilizers, and herbicides), organic cotton is much more expensive to produce and purchase. Is it worth the few extra dollars to know that the environment is not being harmed? Apparently enough people do think so. Farmers growing organic cotton have had a difficult time keeping up with demand since 2000. There are other sustainable fibers that we will likely see more of in the next decade: bamboo, hemp, Tencel (made from wood pulp cellulose), recycled polyester, SeaCell (a blend of cellulose, seaweed substances, and silver), jute. and ramie (http://www.natural-environment.com/blog/2008/04/10/17-eco-friendly-fabrics/).

Learn more about skin care. Be an advocate for safe products. As mentioned earlier, your skin is the largest organ of your body. Take the time to research the products that you use regularly to be sure that the ingredients are actually safe. The skin "care" and cosmetic industries are not regulated by the FDA. Due to the compelling evidence of the toxicity and potential harm caused by certain ingredients in many skin "care" and fragrance products, the Campaign for Safe Cosmetics was launched in 2004 in an effort to keep consumers and workers within the industry safe (http://www.safecosmetics.org/).

Learn More about Energy Consumption

We can conserve energy in numerous ways. Purchasing products that use less energy to produce and transport is one area of conservation that is often overlooked. The United States Department of Energy offers excellent information for consumers (http://www.energy.gov/for-consumers.htm).

Ask Questions. Be an Advocate for Healthful, Sustainable Food and Products—for Your Own Health, the Health of all People, and the Health of the Planet

Never doubt that a small group of thoughtful, committed people can change the world. Indeed, it is the only thing that ever has.

—Margaret Mead.

Test Your Knowledge

Name _____ **Date** _____

1. What is the basic formula for weight loss?

2. What is the basic formula for weight gain?

3. What is the basic formula for maintaining weight?

4. What are the essential nutrients that our body needs?

5. What do the three gunas represent? Please list all three and the qualities of each.

    1.

    2.

    3.

6. **List three sattvic foods.**

    1.

    2.

    3.

7. **Please list three rajasic foods.**

    1.

    2.

    3.

8. **Please list three tamasic foods.**

    1.

    2.

    3.

9. Briefly summarize how to use yogic principles to be a wiser consumer. Please list at least 5 things you can do.

Going Deeper: "OMwork"

In addition to the resources listed within Chapter 10, the list below represents most of the topics within this chapter. You may use them to enhance your knowledge of the subject matter that you find to be of interest.

Movies/Documentaries

- Lee Fulkerson, 2011 *Forks Over Knives*
- Robert Kenner, 2008 *Food, Inc.*
- Chris Taylor, 2008 *Food Fight*
- Aaron Woolf 2007 *King Corn*
- Bill Haney 2007 *The Price of Sugar*
- Nikolaus Geyrhalter 2005 *Our Daily Bread*
- Morgan Spurlock 2004 *Super Size Me*

Books

- Frances Moore Lappe. *Diet for a Small Planet*. Random House Publishing Group 1971 Toronto, Canada
- John Robbins. *Diet for a New America*. H.J. Kramer, 1987
- Pollan, Michael (2001). *The Botany of Desire: A Plant's-Eye View of the World*. New York: Random House. *ISBN 9780375501296.*
- Pollan, Michael (2006). *The Omnivore's Dilemma: A Natural History of Four Meals*. New York: Penguin Press. *ISBN 9781594200823.*
- Pollan, Michael (2008). *In Defense of Food: An Eater's Manifesto*. New York: Penguin Press. *ISBN 9781594201455.*
- Pollan, Michael (2009). *Food Rules: An Eater's Manual*. New York: Penguin Press. *ISBN 9780143116387.*
- Barbara Kingsolver (2007). *Animal, Vegetable, Miracle*. HarperCollins Publishers New York. *ISBN 9780060852559.*

"OMwork"

- ~ *Make an energy conservation agreement with whomever you live with.*
- ~ *Find local farmers markets, and plan which ones you may be able to frequent.*
- ~ *Make a shopping and food prep plan.*
- ~ *Check your local wellness center for a grocery store tour. You can learn a lot from touring a grocery store with a registered dietician or nutritionist.*

Continuing Your Practice

Courtesy of Alison Donley

 End of Semester Questions

Please answer the following questions:

1. Did you have fun learning about Yoga?

2. Did you enjoy learning the physical practice?

3. Did you have improvements on any of the fitness tests? If so, which ones? How much of an improvement did you have?

4. Did you notice an improvement in any of the common symptoms of stress you had been experiencing at the beginning of the semester?

5. Were there any symptoms of stress that you had been experiencing at the beginning of the semester that you now no longer experience?

6. Were you able to notice a difference in your energy level on the day(s) you had yoga class?

7. Did you begin practicing any of the yamas? If so, which ones?

8. Did you begin practicing any niyamas? If so, which ones?

9. Were you able to make any lifestyle changes to support your quest for wellness?

10. Have you experienced any improvement in any of the dimensions of wellness? If so, which ones?

11. Have you used yogic breathing outside of the class? If so, was it helpful?

12. What do you feel has been the most beneficial aspect of this class for you?

13. What was your favorite part of the class?

14. What was your least favorite part of the class?

15. Will you continue to practice yoga?

The Rest Is Up to You

You have worked hard. The semester has provided you with some basic knowledge of yoga practice, now the rest is up to you. If you like the way you feel, by all means, continue. You already have a practice that you know.

There may be plenty of days when you will find it difficult to do a sixty-minute practice, but it is *not* difficult to talk yourself into three Sun Salutations. Roll out your mat. Every day. Even if it is only five mindful minutes of sitting with your breath, do it. If you roll the mat out with the intention of three Sun Salutes, you will likely be inspired to do three more. And then, a few of the standing postures, a few of the seated ones, and so on. Creating a home practice is one of the greatest accomplishments on your path of yoga. Honoring yourself by practicing regularly is a true act of self-respect and self-love.

If you have a particular attraction to Ashtanga vinyasa yoga, find a studio where you can go to practice with like-minded souls. Be sure to find a well-trained instructor. You have gotten only an introduction to this amazing system. Continue by learning the full practice—and remember, your practice will be your greatest teacher.

Courtesy of Rachel Donley

Courtesy of Rachel Donley

Courtesy of Rachel Donley

Courtesy of Rachel Donley

If Ashtanga vinyasa was not your "cup of tea," and you enjoyed the gentle practices more, then look for studios offering those kinds of classes. Within the practice of Hatha yoga, it would be tough to imagine that you would not be able to find something that resonates with you. Find a style that moves you, both physically and mentally.

Yoga as a lifestyle is an option that offers great peace. Imagine living in a state of peace and clarity; not just experiencing it on occasion. Inner peace is what allows us to be peaceful out there in the world. Inner peace in an individual leads to familial peace. Peaceful families become a part a peaceful community. A peaceful community lends itself to a more peaceful state, which leads to a more peaceful nation. Just as fear, anger, and hate can cause a ripple effect, so too can love and peace. It may sound "fluffy," but it is a concept worth exploring. Imagine...

There are many Paths to Wellness. If yoga practice or even Yoga as a lifestyle is not the road you wish to take, keep searching. Find the right path for you, and travel it with intention.

May you BE well on your journey!

Courtesy of Alison Donley

Fitness Assessments

While measuring levels of muscular flexibility and muscular endurance may not be very "yogic" (you are perfect as you are), the following assessments will allow you to clearly see the effect of the physical practice at the end of the semester. Most will be assessed as P (passing) or NPY (not passing yet).

Date				Date			
Hamstrings				Hamstrings			
Right	P	NPY	Degree	Right	P	NPY	Degree
Left	P	NPY	Degree	Left	P	NPY	Degree
Improvement?	R	L					

Not passing yet (NPY) leg < 90 degrees

Passing (P) leg at 90 degrees or more

Both legs need to be completely straight. Keep head, neck, and shoulders relaxed as you gently bicep curl the leg toward the chest. Do not stretch to the point of pain. Stretch should be felt in the hamstrings, not in the buttock or knee. Slowly stretch the leg to your edge. Leg to 90 degrees = passing. Contraindications: Injury to hamstrings or gluteals. Estimate the degree to which you were able to stretch.

Date				Date			
Quadriceps				Quadriceps			
Right	P	NPY	Degree	Right	P	NPY	Degree
Left	P	NPY	Degree	Left	P	NPY	Degree
Improvement?	R	L					

Do not stretch to the point of pain. Stretch should be felt in the quadriceps, not in the knee. From prone position with chin resting on the floor, gently stretch heel toward buttock. Heel to buttock = passing. Contraindications: Injury to quadriceps or hip flexors.

Date				Date			
Hip Flexors				Hip Flexors			
Right	P	NPY	Degree	Right	P	NPY	Degree
Left	P	NPY	Degree	Left	P	NPY	Degree
Improvement?	R	L					

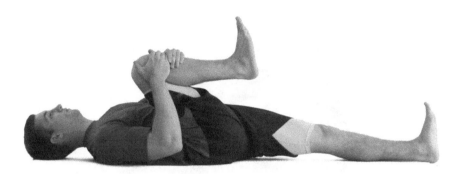

Do not stretch to the point of pain. From prone position, bend one knee in as tight as possible to the chest. For example, when stretching the left hip flexors, the right knee is pulled in and left leg remains straight (passing) or bends (not passing yet). Contraindications: Injury to quadriceps, gluteals, or hip flexors.

Date				Date			
Trunk Rotation				Trunk Rotation			
Right	P	NPY	Degree	Right	P	NPY	Degree
Left	P	NPY	Degree	Left	P	NPY	Degree
Improvement?	R	L					

Do not stretch to the point of pain. Keep shoulders directly over hips and lengthen your spine as you twist. Gently stretch to your edge. A complete one-quarter turn (90 degrees) = passing. Contraindications: Back injury.

Date				Date			
Calves				Calves			
Right	P	NPY	Degree	Right	P	NPY	Degree
Left	P	NPY	Degree	Left	P	NPY	Degree
Improvement?	R	L					

Do not stretch to the point of pain. Either assessing from seated: 70 degrees = passing, or from Downward Dog: heels to floor = passing. Contraindications: Injury to calf muscles or to hamstrings.

Date				Date			
Shoulders				Shoulders			
Right	P	NPY	Degree	Right	P	NPY	Degree
Left	P	NPY	Degree	Left	P	NPY	Degree
Improvement?	R	L					

Do not stretch to the point of pain. Lifting the arm straight up beside the ear, or 180 degrees = passing. Contraindications: Shoulder or triceps injury.

Date			Date		
Push-ups	MP	RP	Push-ups	MP	RP
Improvement?					

Circle MP (above) if you chose to do modified push-ups, and circle RP if you choose to do regular push-ups. Record the number of push-ups you are able to do *without stopping*. Please keep arms directly under shoulders and bend elbows straight back. *Stop* counting when you can no longer maintain form and fluidity. The "pecking chicken" and "the worm" are *not* push-ups!

The pecking chicken   **The worm**

Please answer the following question on the date of the first assessments at the beginning of the semester:

1. What are your fitness intentions for the semester based on the results of the assessments?

Please answer the following question on the date of the last assessments at the end of the semester:

1. Were you able to improve in any of the assessments? Which ones?

Stress Assessments

The list below represents many of the most common physical and emotional symptoms of stress. Please complete the assessment in the beginning of the semester and then once again, near the end of the semester.

Please rate the symptoms in the column to the right. For any that you have been experiencing for the last few weeks, please rank them:

1 = Mild   **2** = Moderate   and   **3** = Severe

Symptom(s) of Stress	Date	Date
Frequent headaches		
Jaw clenching, grinding teeth, jaw or mouth pain		
Stuttering or stammering, trembling hands or mouth		
Neck ache, back pain, neck or back muscle spasms		
Faintness, dizziness, light headedness		
Ringing in the ears		
Blushing, sweating frequently		
Sweaty hands or feet; cold hands or feet		
Difficulty swallowing, dry mouth		
Frequent colds, infections, flare up of herpes sores		
Low grade fevers		
Acne		
Frequent rashes, itching, hives, or "goosebumps"		
Frequent "allergy" attacks, elevated histamine levels		
Frequent heartburn, stomach pain, nausea		
Constipation, diarrhea, frequent urination		
Difficulty breathing, sighing		
Sudden panic attacks		
Excess belching, flatulence		
Heart palpitations, chest pain		
Poor sexual desire or performance		
Excess nervousness, anxiety, worry, guilt		

Symptom(s) of Stress	Date	Date
Increased anger, frustration, hostility		
Difficulty in making decisions		
Depression		
Frequent or wild mood swings		
Poor concentration, confusion, forgetfulness, disorganization		
Feeling overloaded or overwhelmed		
Lack of productivity, inability to complete work efficiently		
Excuses or lies to cover up poor effort		
Insomnia, nightmares, disturbing dreams		
Rapid speech, mumbled speech, or speaking too softly		
Communication difficulties		
Constant weakness, fatigue, tiredness		
Irritability, edginess, increased frustration		
Overreaction to petty annoyances		
Increased smoking, alcohol or drug use		
Increase in other addictive behaviors (gambling, shopping, etc.)		
Increased incidence of minor accidents		
Increase in appetite, overeating, weight gain		
Decrease in appetite, weight loss		
Frequent crying spells		
Compulsive or obsessive actions		
Thoughts of harming oneself, suicidal thoughts		
Feelings of worthlessness, feeling of loneliness		
Little interest in punctuality or appearance		
Nervous habits, racing thoughts, fidgeting		
Defensiveness or suspicion in excess		
Social withdrawal and isolation		
Misuse of over-the-counter drugs		

Adapted from American Institute of Stress.

FOOD & MOOD JOURNALS

Day 1/ Date-				
FOOD What was the food consumed?	Approxlmately how much was consumed?	TIME/PLACE that the food was consumed	SENSORY Were you hungry when you ate the food(s)?	EMOTIONAL How were you feeling emotionally?

How well do you feel that you nourished your body today?

Did the foods you ate give you sufficient energy today?

Approximately how many ounces of water did you drink today?

Please list any additional beverages consumed today.

FOOD & MOOD JOURNALS

Day 2/ Date-				
FOOD What was the food consumed?	Approxlmately how much was consumed?	TIME/PLACE that the food was consumed	SENSORY Were you hungry when you ate the food(s)?	EMOTIONAL How were you feeling emotionally?

How well do you feel that you nourished your body today?

Did the foods you ate give you sufficient energy today?

Approximately how many ounces of water did you drink today?

Please list any additional beverages consumed today.

FOOD & MOOD JOURNALS

FOOD What was the food consumed?	Approximately how much was consumed?	TIME/PLACE that the food was consumed	SENSORY Were you hungry when you ate the food(s)?	EMOTIONAL How were you feeling emotionally?

Day 3/ Date-

How well do you feel that you nourished your body today?

Did the foods you ate give you sufficient energy today?

Approximately how many ounces of water did you drink today?

Please list any additional beverages consumed today.

FOOD & MOOD JOURNALS

Day 4/ Date-				
FOOD What was the food consumed?	Approximately how much was consumed?	TIME/PLACE that the food was consumed	SENSORY Were you hungry when you ate the food(s)?	EMOTIONAL How were you feeling emotionally?

How well do you feel that you nourished your body today?

Did the foods you ate give you sufficient energy today?

Approximately how many ounces of water did you drink today?

Please list any additional beverages consumed today.

FOOD & MOOD JOURNALS

Day 5/ Date-				
FOOD What was the food consumed?	Approximately how much was consumed?	TIME/PLACE that the food was consumed	SENSORY Were you hungry when you ate the food(s)?	EMOTIONAL How were you feeling emotionally?

How well do you feel that you nourished your body today?

Did the foods you ate give you sufficient energy today?

Approximately how many ounces of water did you drink today?

Please list any additional beverages consumed today.

FOOD & MOOD JOURNALS

Day 6/ Date-				
FOOD What was the food consumed?	Approximately how much was consumed?	TIME/PLACE that the food was consumed	SENSORY Were you hungry when you ate the food(s)?	EMOTIONAL How were you feeling emotionally?

How well do you feel that you nourished your body today?

Did the foods you ate give you sufficient energy today?

Approximately how many ounces of water did you drink today?

Please list any additional beverages consumed today.

FOOD & MOOD JOURNALS

Day 7/ Date-				
FOOD What was the food consumed?	Approximately how much was consumed?	TIME/PLACE that the food was consumed	SENSORY Were you hungry when you ate the food(s)?	EMOTIONAL How were you feeling emotionally?

How well do you feel that you nourished your body today?

Did the foods you ate give you sufficient energy today?

Approximately how many ounces of water did you drink today?

Please list any additional beverages consumed today.

FOOD & MOOD JOURNALS

Day 8/ Date-				
FOOD What was the food consumed?	Approxlmately how much was consumed?	TIME/PLACE that the food was consumed	SENSORY Were you hungry when you ate the food(s)?	EMOTIONAL How were you feeling emotionally?

How well do you feel that you nourished your body today?

Did the foods you ate give you sufficient energy today?

Approximately how many ounces of water did you drink today?

Please list any additional beverages consumed today.

FOOD & MOOD JOURNALS

Day 9/ Date-				
FOOD What was the food consumed?	Approximately how much was consumed?	TIME/PLACE that the food was consumed	SENSORY Were you hungry when you ate the food(s)?	EMOTIONAL How were you feeling emotionally?

How well do you feel that you nourished your body today?

Did the foods you ate give you sufficient energy today?

Approximately how many ounces of water did you drink today?

Please list any additional beverages consumed today.

FOOD & MOOD JOURNALS

Day 10/ Date-				
FOOD What was the food consumed?	Approximately how much was consumed?	TIME/PLACE that the food was consumed	SENSORY Were you hungry when you ate the food(s)?	EMOTIONAL How were you feeling emotionally?

How well do you feel that you nourished your body today?

Did the foods you ate give you sufficient energy today?

Approximately how many ounces of water did you drink today?

Please list any additional beverages consumed today.

FOOD & MOOD JOURNALS

FOOD What was the food consumed?	Approximately how much was consumed?	TIME/PLACE that the food was consumed	SENSORY Were you hungry when you ate the food(s)?	EMOTIONAL How were you feeling emotionally?

Day 11/ Date-

How well do you feel that you nourished your body today?

Did the foods you ate give you sufficient energy today?

Approximately how many ounces of water did you drink today?

Please list any additional beverages consumed today.

FOOD & MOOD JOURNALS

Day 12/ Date-				
FOOD What was the food consumed?	Approximately how much was consumed?	TIME/PLACE that the food was consumed	SENSORY Were you hungry when you ate the food(s)?	EMOTIONAL How were you feeling emotionally?

How well do you feel that you nourished your body today?

Did the foods you ate give you sufficient energy today?

Approximately how many ounces of water did you drink today?

Please list any additional beverages consumed today.

FOOD & MOOD JOURNALS

Day 13/ Date-				
FOOD What was the food consumed?	Approximately how much was consumed?	TIME/PLACE that the food was consumed	SENSORY Were you hungry when you ate the food(s)?	EMOTIONAL How were you feeling emotionally?

How well do you feel that you nourished your body today?

Did the foods you ate give you sufficient energy today?

Approximately how many ounces of water did you drink today?

Please list any additional beverages consumed today.

FOOD & MOOD JOURNALS

Day 14/ Date-				
FOOD What was the food consumed?	Approximately how much was consumed?	TIME/PLACE that the food was consumed	SENSORY Were you hungry when you ate the food(s)?	EMOTIONAL How were you feeling emotionally?

How well do you feel that you nourished your body today?

Did the foods you ate give you sufficient energy today?

Approximately how many ounces of water did you drink today?

Please list any additional beverages consumed today.

JOURNALS

Week 1

Intention:

Pre- (how I feel before practice)

Post- (how I feel after practice)

Intention:

Pre-

Post-

JOURNALS

Week 2

Intention:

Pre-

Post-

Intention:

Pre-

Post-

JOURNALS

Week 3

Intention:

Pre-

Post-

Intention:

Pre-

Post-

JOURNALS

Week 4
Intention:

Pre-

Post-

Intention:

Pre-

Post-

JOURNALS

Week 5

    Intention:

    Pre-

    Post-

    Intention:

    Pre-

    Post-

JOURNALS

Week 6

Intention:

Pre-

Post-

Intention:

Pre-

Post-

JOURNALS

Week 7

Intention:

Pre-

Post-

Intention:

Pre-

Post-

JOURNALS

Week 8

Intention:

Pre-

Post-

Intention:

Pre-

Post-

JOURNALS

Week 9

Intention:

Pre-

Post-

Intention:

Pre-

Post-

JOURNALS

Week 10

Intention:

Pre-

Post-

Intention:

Pre-

Post-

JOURNALS

Week 11

Intention:

Pre-

Post-

Intention:

Pre-

Post-

JOURNALS

Week 12

Intention:

Pre-

Post-

Intention:

Pre-

Post-

JOURNALS

Week 13

Intention:

Pre-

Post-

Intention:

Pre-

Post-

JOURNALS

Week 14

Intention:

Pre-

Post-

Intention:

Pre-

Post-

JOURNALS

Week 15

Intention:

Pre-

Post-

Intention:

Pre-

Post-

OMWORK JOURNALS

_____

_____

_____

_____

_____

_____

_____

_____

_____

_____

_____

_____

_____

OMWORK JOURNALS

_____

_____

_____

_____

_____

_____

_____

_____

_____

_____

_____

_____

_____

_____

_____

_____

_____

OMWORK JOURNALS

_____

_____

_____

_____

_____

_____

_____

_____

_____

_____

_____

_____

_____

_____

_____

OMWORK JOURNALS

_____
_____
_____
_____
_____
_____
_____
_____
_____
_____
_____
_____
_____
_____
_____
_____
_____

OMWORK JOURNALS

Resources

Introduction

Elizabeth Gilbert. 2006. *Eat, Pray, Love*. Penguin Books. New York, New York Page 122

Alan W. Watts. 1951. *The Wisdom of Insecurity: A Message for an Age of Anxiety* Pantheon Books. New York, New York Page 32

Jon Kabat-Zinn. 1990 *Full Catastrophe Living* Delta, McHenry, Illinois

B.K.S. Iyengar. 1966 *Light on Yoga*, Schocken Books New York, New York

Purpose

David Lynch. 2006. *Catching the Big Fish: Meditation, Consciousness, and Creativity*. Penguin Publishing, New York, New York. Introduction

Chapter 1

Opening quote: Vālmīki (2000). *The Yoga-Vāsistha of Vālmīki*. trans. Vihārilāla Mitra. Delhi: Parimal Publications. Delhi, India OCLC 53149153

Sivananda Yoga Vedanta Center. 1983. *The Sivananda Companion to Yoga*. Fireside, New York, New York, from the Foreward

B.K.S. Iyengar. 2005. *Light on Life: The Yoga Journey to Wholeness, Inner Peace, and Ultimate Freedom*. Rodale Publishers, Emmaus, PA Page 3

Peter Russell and Alistair Shearer. 1978. Translation of *The Upanishads* Bell Tower, New York, New York

Beryl Bender Birch. 2000. *Beyond Power Yoga*. Fireside, New York, New York Page 37

Eckhart Tolle, 1997. *The Power of Now: A Guide to Spiritual Enlightenment*. Namaste Publishing, Canada

Mark Singleton. 2010. *Yoga Body: The Origins of Modern Posture Practice*. Oxford University Press, Inc. New York, New York from the Introduction

Websites for Sanskrit information:

    http://www.indopedia.org

    http://www.americansanskrit.com

Resources for Information on Philosophy and History of Yoga:

    http://www.swamij.com/yoga-sutras.htm

    http://www.americanyogaassociation.org

    http://www.newworldencyclopedia.org

    http://www.yogajournal.com/wisdom/tradition and history

    http://www.fas.harvard.edu/~pluralsm/affiliates/jainism/jainedu/yoga.htm

    http://www.sivananda.org

Phil Catalfo. 2001. "Is Yoga a Religion?" *Yoga Journal* (March/April): www.yogajournal.com/lifestyle/283

Gita Desai. 2004. *Yoga Unveiled: Evolution and Essence of a Spiritual Tradition.* Documentary.

> http://www.kym.org/sub_abt_ourteacher.html

> http://www.swamij.com/swami-vivekananda-1893.htm

> http://www.kpjayi.org

> http://www.time.com/time/magazine/article/0,9171,994041,00.html

> http://www.nytimes.com/2008/02/07/arts/music/07yogi.html

> http://www.swamisatchidananda.org/docs2/woodstock.htm

Swami Svatmarama. 2002. (English Trans. by Brian Dana Akers). *The Hatha Yoga Pradipika: The Original Sanskrit* (**YogaVidya.com**). Woodstock, New York

Chapter 2

Peter Matthiessen. 1996. *The Snow Leopard.* Penguin Books. New York New York

> http://news.stanford.edu/news/2009/august24/multitask-research-study-082409.html

> http://www.brainandhealth.com/Brain-Waves.html

> http://www.yogapoint.com/info/research5.htm

> http://www.poetseers.org/nobel_prize_for_literature/tagore/short/lept/

David Korten. "We Are Hard Wired to Care and Connect." 2008. *Yes!* magazine (July):

> http://www.yesmagazine.org/issues/purple-america/we-are-hard-wired-to-care-and-connect

Marc Kauffman. 2005. "Meditation Gives Brain a Charge, Study Finds." *Washington Post* (January 3, 2005) page A 05

Dr. Timothy McCall. "The Scientific Basis for Yoga Therapy." *Yoga Journal:* http://www.yogajournal.com/for_teachers/2016

> http://www.thehealthcenter.info/adult-stress/types-of-stress.htm

> http://www.dealwithstress.com/Types-Of-Stress.html

> http://www.stress.org/topic-effects.htm

> www.yogasite.com

Paramhansa Yogananda. 1946 *Autobiography of a Yogi.* Free Press New York, New York

Dr. Dean Ornish 1990 *Reversing Heart Disease* Ballantine Books New York, New York

Vishnu-Devananda wrote one of the contemporary yoga classics, *The Complete Illustrated Book of Yoga.* First published in 1960

Norman Cousins 1979 *Anatomy of an Illness*, W. W. Norton and Company, Inc. New York, New York

Article on Laughter Yoga: http://www.odemagazine.com/doc/65/medicine-of-mirth

Chapter 3

B.K.S. Iyengar quote: http://www.quotegarden.com/health.html

Werner Hoeger and Sharon Hoeger. 2007. *Fitness and Wellness.* Thomson Wadsworth, Belmont, CA Page 153 and page 160

National Institutes of Health website: http://www.nih.gov/

National Wellness Institute Website: http://www.nationalwellness.org/

Alisa Bauman. 2002."Is Yoga Enough to Keep You Fit?" *Yoga Journal* (September/October): http://www.yogajournal.com/practice/739?print=1

Chapter 4

Amy Novotney. 2009. "Yoga as a Practice Tool." *Monitor on Psychology* (November): http://www.apa.org/monitor/2009/11/yoga.aspx

Swami Chetadananda. 1995. *Will I Be the Hero of My Own Life?* Rudra Press. Portland, Oregon

Amy Weintraub. 2004. *Yoga for Depression*. Broadway Books. New York, New York

http://www.health.harvard.edu/newsletters/Harvard_Mental_Health_Letter/2009/April/Yoga-for-anxiety-and-depression

http://www.psychologytoday.com/articles/200011/yoga-not-just-exercise

http://www.yogajournal.com/for_teachers/2390

http://www.abc-of-yoga.com/yoga-and-health/yoga-for-anxiety.asp

http://www.yogajournal.com/lifestyle/894

Chapter 5

Opening quote: Frank Scully quote: http://www.quotationspage.com/quote/2469.html

Imagine lyrics: http://www.metrolyrics.com/imagine-lyrics-john-lennon.html

Eisenhower quote: http://harpers.org/archive/2007/11/hbc-90001660

Buddha Quote: http://www.goodreads.com/quotes/show/35064

Johanna Maheshvari Mosca, PhD. 2000. *YogaLife: 10 Steps to Freedom*. Sedona Spirit Yoga Publications, Sedona, AZ

Ecknath Easwaran. 1977. *The Mantram Handbook*. The Blue Mountain Center of Meditation. Tomales, CA Page 154

Gita Desai. 2004. *Yoga Unveiled: Evolution and Essence of a Spiritual Tradition*. Documentary.

Cat De Rham and Michelle Gill. 2001. *The Spirit of Yoga*. Thorsons, Rochester, Vermont Page 30

Osho International Foundation 2002 *Everday Osho* Fair Winds Press, Gloucester, MA Page 4, "*An Echoing Place*"

Louise Hay. 1999. "Power Thought Cards" www.hayhouse.com, Carlsbad, CA

Rilke Quote: http://www.univforum.org/pdf/4311979_Rilke_poet_1001_ENG.pdf

Shiva Rea. "The Practice of Surrender": http://www.yogajournal.com/wisdom/776

Robert Svoboda and Scott Blossom. January/February 2007 "Steadiness & Ease: Balancing Ourselves in 'Good Space'" http://www.himalayaninstitute.org/yogaplus/Article.aspx?id=3011

David Swenson. February, 2010. Workshop Series: Ashtanga Yoga: Inside and Out

Beryl Bender Birch. 2000. *Beyond Power Yoga*. Fireside, New York, New York Page 179

Acronym for FEAR (www.essentialawareness.org/neale-donald-walsch-discusses-the-emotion-of-fear.php–United Kingdom):

Dogen quote: http://www.irealm.org/quotes/dispquote.php?page=d

Sai Baba quote: http://www.mindbodyspiritjournal.com/324/before-you-speak-ask-yourself/

Gandhi quote: http://thinkexist.com/quotes/mahatma_gandhi/

Chapter 6

Quote by Lao Tzu from *The Tao Te Ching.* http://www.quotationspage.com/quote/24004.html

Sivananda Yoga Vedanta Center. 1983. *The Sivananda Companion to Yoga.* Fireside, New York, New York, page 68

Beryl Bender Birch. 2000. *Beyond Power Yoga.* Fireside, New York, New York Page 58

David Swenson. 1999. *Ashtanga Yoga: The Practice Manual: An Illustrated Guide to Personal Practice.* Ashtanga Yoga Productions Austin, TX Pages 9–10 and page 12

Chapter 7

Quote by Meher Baba from: Ecknath Easwaran. 1977. *The Mantram Handbook.* The Blue Mountain Center of Meditation. Tomales, CA Page 80

David Swenson. 1999. *Ashtanga Yoga: The Practice Manual: An Illustrated Guide To Personal Practice.* Ashtanga Yoga Productions Austin, TX Page 21

Chapter 8

Dykema, Ravi. *Yoga for Fitness and Wellness.* Canada: Thomson Wadsworth, 2006

Gates, Rolf, and Katrina Kenison. *Meditations from the Mat: Daily Reflections on the Path of Yoga.* New York: Random House, 2002

Hall, Dr. Kathleen. *A Life in Balance: Nourishing the Four Roots of True Happiness.* New York: American Management Associations, 2006

Khalsa, Gurucharan Singh, Ph.D., and Yogi Bhajan, Ph.D. *Breathwalk: Breathing Your Way to a Revitalized Body, Mind, and Spirit.* New York: Broadway Books, 2000

Lasater, Judith, Ph.D., P.T. *Relax and Renew: Restful Yoga for Stressful Times.* Rodmell, 1995

Pizer, Ann. "Ocean Breath, Ujjayi Pranayama." About.com, 2006

Chapter 9

Dykema, Ravi. *Yoga for Fitness and Wellness.* Canada: Thomson Wadsworth, 2006

Fried, Dr. Robert, and Joseph Grimaldi. *Psychology and Physiology of Breathing.* New York: Springer, 2005

Gates, Rolf, and Katrina Kenison. *Meditations form the Mat: Daily Reflections on the Path of Yoga.* New York: Random House, 2002

Hall, Dr. Kathleen. *A Life in Balance: Nourishing the Four Roots of True Happiness.* New York: American Management Association, 2006

Holistic.com: "Health Conditions That Are Benefited by Meditation," 2006

Khalsa, Gurucharan Singh, Ph.D., and Yogi Bhajan, Ph.D. *Breathwalk: Breathing Your Way to a Revitalized Body, Mind, and Spirit.* New York: Broadway Books, 2000

Lasater, Judith, Ph.D., P.T. *Relax and Renew: Restful Yoga for Stressful Times.* Rodmell, 1995

Moyer, Bill. *Healing and the Mind.* New York: Doubleday, 1993

Piver, Susan. *Joyful Mind: A Practical Guide to Buddhist Meditation.* China: Rodale Inc., 2002

Pizer, Ann. "Ocean Breath, Ujjayi Pranayama." About.com, 2006

Tulku, Tarthang. *Tibetan Meditation: Practical Teachings and Step-By-Step Exercises on How to Live in Harmony, Peace, and Happiness.* London: Duncan Baird Publishers, 2006

Zinn-Kabat, Jon. *Wherever You Go There You Are: Mindfulness Meditation In Everyday Life.* New York: Hyperion Books, 1994

Chapter 10

Bill Cosby. 2003. *I Am What I Ate…and I'm frightened.* HarperCollins New York, New York

"Prevalence and Trends in Obesity Among U.S. Adults, 1999–2008." 2010. *Journal of the American Medical Association* (January). Pages 235–241

Eric Schlosser. 2002. *Fast Food Nation: The Dark Side of the All-American Meal.* HarperCollins, New York, New York

http://www.cdc.gov/nutrition/everyone/basics/foodgroups.html

www.mypryamid.gov

http://www.mayoclinic.com/health/vegetarian-diet/hq01596

"In Your Face." May, 2010. *Nutrition Action Healthletter.* Pages 3–7.

Gandhi quote on moral progress of a society: www.quotegarden.com

Sivananda Yoga Vedanta Center. 1983. *The Sivananda Companion to Yoga.* Fireside, New York, New York, page 78

www.foodroutes.org

www.buylocalpa.org

www.localharvest.org

www.eatwellguide.org

www.rodaleinstitute.org/farm_locator

http://www.youtube.com/watch?v=IOYhM2c8PmM

http://www.sustainabletable.org/home.php

http://www.greenamericatoday.org/

http://www.ams.usda.gov/AMSv1.0/cool

http://www.edf.org/page.cfm?tagID=1521

http://www.humanesociety.org

http://www.eatwild.com/basics.html

http://rodaleinstitute.org

http://www.ams.usda.gov/AMSv1.0/nop

http://www.ewg.org

"Fear of Fresh." December, 2006. *Nutrition Action Healthletter* http://www.cspinet.org

Centers for Disease Control and Prevention. 2009. *Morbidity and Mortality Weekly Report.* (March 27, 2009). Pages 281–283

http://www.princeton.edu/main/news/archive/S26/91/22K07/

http://www.mayoclinic.com/health/fiber/nu00033

Greenerchoices.org, 2007

http://www.worldwatch.org/node/1499

http://www.panna.org/resources/cotton

http://www.natural-environment.com/blog/2008/04/10/17-eco-friendly-fabrics/

http://www.safecosmetics.org/

http://www.energy.gov/forconsumers.htm

Chapter 11

Fitness Assessments

Stress Assessments

50 Common symptoms of Stress adapted from **http://www.Stress.org**

CPSIA information can be obtained
at www.ICGtesting.com
Printed in the USA
LVHW01s0048240718
584690LV00001B/1/P